This book provided
courtesy of

Office of the Secretary of State
Washington State Library

funded in part by

INSTITUTE of
Museum and Library
SERVICES

A GANNETT COMPANY

Lifeline
BIOGRAPHIES

SUZANNE COLLINS
Words on Fire

by Marcia Amidon Lusted

Twenty-First Century Books · Minneapolis

Copyright © 2013 by Lerner Publishing Group, Inc.

Twenty-First Century Books
A division of Lerner Publishing Group, Inc.
241 First Avenue North
Minneapolis, MN 55401 U.S.A.

Website address: www.lernerbooks.com

Library of Congress Cataloging-in-Publication Data

Lusted, Marcia Amidon.
    Suzanne Collins : words on fire / by Marcia Amidon Lusted.
        p.   cm. — (USA Today lifeline biographies)
    Includes bibliographical references and index.
    ISBN 978–0–7613–8638–4 (lib. bdg. : alk. paper)
    1. Collins, Suzanne—Juvenile literature. 2. Authors, American—20th century—Biography—Juvenile literature. I. Title.
    PS3603.O4558Z75 2013
    813'.6—dc23 [B]   2011045487

Manufactured in the United States of America
1 – PP – 7/15/12

![USA TODAY A GANNETT COMPANY] | Lifeline BIOGRAPHIES

USA TODAY
A GANNETT COMPANY

INTRODUCTION

The trilogy: The first book in Suzanne Collins's trilogy featured heroine Katniss Everdeen in a dreary future. The film rights were optioned by movie studio Lionsgate. Fans followed the movie production closely, hoping their favorite characters would be perfectly cast.

Hungry for Entertainment

In March 2011, the biggest news in the entertainment world was the casting of a movie called *The Hunger Games*. The movie would be based on the first book in a best-selling trilogy by author Suzanne Collins. The film studio Lionsgate bought the movie rights to *The Hunger Games* just six months after the book was published in 2008. The president of Lionsgate said, "This is exactly the kind of movie I came to Lionsgate to make: youthful, exciting, smart and edgy. We are looking forward to . . . creating a movie that satisfies audiences' hunger for high-quality entertainment."

By early 2011, excitement over the movie was growing. Casting began with the announcement that Oscar-nominated actor Jennifer Lawrence would play the role of Katniss Everdeen, the leading character in *The Hunger Games*. Even though some

Katniss casting: Actress Jennifer Lawrence was one of the first people cast in the *The Hunger Games* movie. She dyed her blonde hair dark brown to look more like the character of Katniss.

fans felt Lawrence wasn't the best choice for the role, Collins herself said, "Jennifer's just an incredible actress. So powerful, vulnerable, beautiful, unforgiving and brave. I never thought we'd find somebody this perfect for the role. And I can't wait for everyone to see her play it."

June 30, 2011

Book Buzz

From the Pages of
<u>USA TODAY</u>

'Hunger' strikes: The movie version of *The Hunger Games*, starring Jennifer Lawrence, won't be released until March. But thanks in part to growing online chatter about the film and its cast, all three titles in Suzanne Collins's teen series, set in a dystopian future, are in the list's top 10. *Games*, released in 2008, is No. 4. *Catching Fire* (2009) is No. 8, and *Mockingjay* (2010) is No. 10. Publisher Scholastic reports 9.6 million copies in print. A $30 gift edition of *The Hunger Games* will be released in November, with three movie tie-in versions out in February. Another factor driving sales: *Games* is showing up on high school summer reading lists, which now include more contemporary options for students.

—Deirdre Donahue; Bob Minzesheimer; Carol Memmott

Book to movie: Movie tie-in editions of *The Hunger Games*, as well as other movie merchandise such as T-shirts, were available to fans of the books.

Finding Peeta and Gale: Suzanne Collins poses with Josh Hutcherson *(left)* and Liam Hemsworth *(right)* at the premiere of *The Hunger Games* movie in March 2012. Hutcherson plays Peeta in the film, and Hemsworth was cast as Gale.

The other principal characters in the movie were soon cast, with Liam Hemsworth as Gale and Josh Hutcherson as Peeta. Suzanne Collins and director Gary Ross wrote the screenplay, and filming began in North Carolina in late spring of 2011. The movie was set to release on March 23, 2012. Fans eagerly awaited every bit of news about the movie's cast and the filming locations.

The World of the Games

The Hunger Games story centers on Katniss Everdeen, a sixteen-year-old girl who lives in a futuristic setting. The United States has been through a destructive war in which many Americans were killed. A new central government known as the Capitol rules the nation's twelve districts. Food and resources are scarce. Like almost everyone else in this society, Katniss and her friend Gale must hunt and scavenge to find enough food to feed their families.

To keep the population under control and remind them of the government's authority, the Capitol requires each district to hold a yearly lottery known as the Reaping. Through the lottery, a boy and a girl are chosen to compete in the annual Hunger Games. The Games is an event in which the twenty-four tributes, or contestants, fight to the death in a large arena, which is different every year. The Games are broadcast live on television, not unlike the reality shows of the twenty-first century. The brutal competition ends when all but one contestant has been killed. The surviving tribute is then declared the winner of the Games.

When the lottery takes place in her district, Katniss's little sister, Prim, is chosen. Horrified at the thought of sending her sister to the Games, Katniss volunteers to take her place. Peeta, the other tribute from her district, is a boy she barely knows but who has helped her in the past. She participates in the Games, where she has to find a way

The Reaping: In a scene from *The Hunger Games* movie, Katniss *(center)*, played by Jennifer Lawrence, waits to hear the names of the District 12 tributes during the Reaping ceremony.

to survive and return home to her mother and sister. Katniss not only survives the Games, she also forges a close bond with Peeta after he is injured during the competition in the arena. Even though the rules of the Games allow for only one winner, Katniss and Peeta refuse to kill each other. Instead, they threaten to kill themselves unless the government accepts them both as victors.

After the release of *The Hunger Games* novel, young adult and adult fans—both male and female—eagerly awaited the release of the next two books in the trilogy (*Catching Fire* in 2009 and *Mockingjay* in 2010). All three books appeared on every major best-seller list. *Mockingjay* sold 450,000 copies in its first week of release alone. The Hunger Games series came at just the right time to fill readers' need for something new. In fact, critics compared the Hunger Games trilogy to the earlier successes of the Harry Potter and Twilight series and their authors. Even Twilight series author Stephenie Meyer called Collins's books amazing.

More than 9.6 million copies of the Hunger Games books are in print. As *People* magazine said, "Collins expertly blends fantasy, romance and political intrigue (so who needs vampires?)."

Book fan: Twilight series author Stephenie Meyer *(above)*, another young-adult fiction writer, said she loved Suzanne Collins's Hunger Games trilogy.

School Library Journal, a magazine for school librarians, described the books' appeal to young readers, saying, "Collins's characters are completely realistic and sympathetic as they form alliances and friendships in the face of overwhelming odds; the plot is tense, dramatic, and engrossing. This book will definitely resonate with the generation raised on reality shows like *Survivor* and *American Gladiator*." School librarians could not keep enough copies of the books on the shelf to satisfy their readers' demands.

Everyone wanted to know more about the author. But Suzanne Collins was not comfortable with her new celebrity status, even though she was not new to publishing. She was already the author of a five-book series called the Underland Chronicles. This series is about a boy who falls through a manhole into an underground world. The series had received many positive reviews.

Collins had also worked as a writer for children's television

In the spotlight: As her books became more popular, Collins found herself sought after by the media and fans. Here she wears a mockingjay necklace during an interview in 2009, before *Catching Fire* was released.

shows on the Nickelodeon channel and had published several companion books. But she was reclusive and didn't like to give interviews or talk about her personal life. The Hunger Games series changed all that. As her books became huge best sellers, fans clamored for more about Suzanne Collins. She had entered a whole new world as a celebrity author. Just like that of her character Katniss, Collins's life would never be the same after *The Hunger Games.*

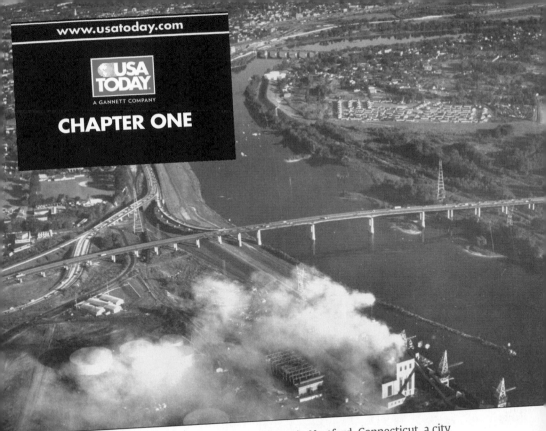

Hails from Hartford: Suzanne Collins was born in Hartford, Connecticut, a city situated on the Connecticut River.

Before The Hunger Games

Suzanne Collins doesn't like to talk about herself. As a result, not a lot is known about her childhood. She was born on August 11, 1962, in Hartford, Connecticut. Her father was in the U.S. Air Force, and the family moved often. They lived in the eastern United States as well as in Europe. Suzanne was the youngest of four and has two sisters and one brother. In 1968, when Suzanne was only six years old, the air force sent her father to Vietnam to fight in the war there between U.S.-backed anti-Communist forces and the North Vietnamese Communist army. "If your parent is deployed [sent to war] and you are that young, you spend the whole time wondering where they are and waiting for them to come home," she remembers. She also remembers that he suffered from horrible nightmares after he came back from Vietnam. She would sometimes wake up to hear him crying out during those dreams.

As she grew up, Suzanne became a typical tween. She liked gymnastics, reading, and running in the woods with her friends near the family's home. She credits her fifth- and sixth-grade English teacher, Miss Vance, with helping her learn to love reading and writing.

IN F⊕CUS

Suzanne Collins's Favorite Books

Entertainment Weekly asked Suzanne Collins what her favorite books are. As a child she loved these books:

Boris by Jaap ter Haar
D'Aulaires' Book of Greek Myths by Ingri and Edgar Parin D'Aulaire
Myths and Enchantment Tales by Margaret Evans Price
The Phantom Tollbooth by Norton Juster
A Wrinkle in Time by Madeleine L'Engle

As an adult, her favorite books are these:

Germinal by Émile Zola
The Heart Is a Lonely Hunter by Carson McCullers
Lord of the Flies by William Golding
A Moveable Feast by Ernest Hemingway
1984 by George Orwell
A Tree Grows in Brooklyn by Betty Smith
We Have Always Lived in the Castle by Shirley Jackson

The Lessons of Vietnam Now Hit Home

From the Pages of
USA TODAY
The United States' involvement in the Vietnam War ended 20 years ago Sunday. It was a conflict that forever altered America's psyche [spirit], split families, alienated friends, put an end to innocence. Now, after two decades, schools are beginning to instruct their students about the war in realistic, sometimes painful ways; many middle-aged teachers still struggle to keep their own emotional wounds from the war out of the classrooms. Combat veteran Larry Rottmann, 51, has returned to Vietnam 16 times in his role as a "witness" to history. His focus is the Vietnamese. Two years ago the Southwest Missouri State University professor went by bicycle and train from Hanoi to Ho Chi Minh City (Saigon) to absorb their culture. But he will not talk much about his first trip—his year with the 25th infantry division in 1967-1968.

Wounded during the 1968 Tet Offensive, Rottmann received a Bronze Star and a Purple Heart. The names of 24 friends are on the Vietnam Veterans Memorial [in Washington, D.C.]. "I did what I was told to do, and I did it the best I could. And then I came back home. I really don't like to discuss personal things." He has emerged from his experiences ardently [passionately] anti-war. Rottmann does not, he says, "tell war stories. I tell cultural stories." His passion is teaching Vietnamese literature and culture. In 1985, he co-founded the Southeast Asia-Ozark Project, organizing courses and seminars at other schools. He travels America teaching the Vietnam War to students as young as elementary school. He is still struck by the geography of the country where Americans and Vietnamese shed so much blood. "It is absolutely spectacular, extraordinarily beautiful."

Recalling downtimes between battles, Rottmann says quiet images of peace would float in his mind. He would record "snippets of songs and poems." It was "the quiet of Vietnam that stayed with me—the silence—more than the noise of the cannons and helicopters." And—"Then came the questions. `Who are these people? Where did they come from? Where did they get their grit?'"

Becoming a teacher was the direct result of his Vietnam experiences. "What is there to understand about war? It is terribly cruel, stupidly violent. But war isn't the

Tour of duty: A U.S. Air Force transport plane drops troops off in Vietnam in 1966. Like these soldiers, Collins's father was sent to fight in this Asian country during the war between the United States and the North Vietnamese.

enemy; ignorance is. And once you believe ignorance is bad, the most direct way to overcome it is to teach."

By the end of Tet, Rottmann says, "Everybody had figured out the war was a bad idea. Many vets going back were having lots of trouble." Rottmann "stayed busy, developed future teaching goals; that was my way of coping, so I didn't descend into drugs and alcohol."

Rottmann now believes the war "will remain forever in the consciousness of the nation." But he worries it will "be misinterpreted." The legacy of Vietnam "all seems to be told from a white male American point of view. The Vietnamese have been left out of the picture for various political, personal and geopolitical reasons."

The kids he teaches know that instinctively, he says. "They do not have the emotional baggage of people from my generation. They ask the key question: `Why did we hate the Vietnamese?'"

He also talks about the fallout on Americans who served. "One of my students said her neighbor cried every time he mowed his lawn," he says. After studying Vietnam, the student finally quizzed her friend. "He told her the sound of the mower always reminded him of [military] helicopters."

Rottmann is not, he says, obsessed with Vietnam. But he does need to teach about it "for my personal peace of mind."

—Karen S. Peterson

"On rainy days, she would take whoever was interested over to the side and read us Edgar Allan Poe stories. She didn't think we were too young to hear it. And we were riveted. That made a huge impression on me." Some of Suzanne's favorite books then included *A Tree Grows in Brooklyn* by Betty Smith, George Orwell's *1984*, and *A Wrinkle in Time* by Madeleine L'Engle.

Poe fan: Collins had a teacher in grade school who helped her develop a love of reading and writing. She introduced Collins to the writing of Edgar Allan Poe *(above)*, a nineteenth-century American author.

Lessons from Dad

Suzanne credits her dad— who is now dead—with teaching her about history and especially about the horrific effects of war. He had a doctorate (PhD) in political science and had taught history at West Point, a prestigious U.S. Army military college in West Point, New York. "It wasn't enough to visit a battlefield," she said. He shared his passion for military history with his family. "We needed to know why the battle occurred, how it played out, and the consequences." The knowledge she gained from her father and his experiences taught her that a war, such as the conflict in Vietnam, can determine a family's fate. She learned that a war affects not only the individual who actually experiences it. In Suzanne's family, her father's trauma, his nightmares, and his obsession with

History buff: Collins's father taught history at West Point military college *(shown above)* in New York. His family learned about war firsthand from him through his own experiences in Vietnam and tours of military battlefields.

military battle history would also affect their family life. She saw firsthand what war had done to her father emotionally. This, in turn, influenced how she felt about war.

As a child, she struggled to deal with her father's memories of violence. War was a firsthand experience in her family, not just something she saw in the news or read about in history books. Her father's need to understand battles and military history meant that his children would also learn about these same things. In fact, violence, recovering from horrible memories of violence, and living with the sorrow of having an absent parent are all themes that are a big part of *The Hunger Games*.

December 13, 2005

War's trauma wears on the children left behind; Pentagon programs aim to soothe anxieties of the young ones whose moms or dads are away at war

From the Pages of
USA TODAY

A squirming audience of pigtails and freckles strains to watch puppets wearing goofy expressions at Bill Hefner Elementary School. At any other school, this might be a holiday pageant or a Thanksgiving play. But not here, in the shadow of the Army's Fort Bragg [in North Carolina], during a war [in Iraq and Afghanistan] that keeps whisking away the moms and the dads of these kids for what seems like forever. The puppet show, wishfully titled *Nothing to Worry About*, is an Army-sponsored program intended to make children of soldiers more resilient by gently reassuring them that their absent parents still love and remember them. Moderator Breta Sandifer reminds the 60 kids that other children share their fears and that talking about them is good. "It's absolutely OK just to cry," she says.

Programs like this are part of a sweeping Pentagon [headquarters of the U.S. Department of Defense] effort to emotionally safeguard children whose parents are at war. An estimated 1.9 million kids have a mom or dad in uniform, and since 2001, a third of all U.S. forces have served or are serving in Iraq or Afghanistan. By helping to care for the families on the home front, officials hope to encourage soldiers to reenlist. They also hope to ensure that a generation of children will better cope with the effects of war. Even as the resources grow, however, military researchers remain concerned. They admit that they're still struggling to understand the impact that the long and repeated battle tours have on the children of those fighting. Previous studies focused on children of a parent gone for a single tour of duty. In this war, families have been separated two, three or more times.

Ten-year-old Kalysta Fern, who lives with her family in Missoula, Mont., began suffering nightmares when her stepfather was deployed [sent] to Iraq from 2003 to 2004. In the dreams, he dies. "'Would he be killed?' That was my most-often

Kids at home: Children who have parents in the military listen to a second-grade peer talk about her own experiences with a parent overseas. The program, sponsored by the Pentagon, is meant to help kids talk about their anxieties in tough times.

question," she recalls. "My mom just told me that she didn't know, but that he probably wouldn't be. . . . When you love someone as much as I love him, it just aches." Bad dreams continue to this day, more than a year after his safe return, she says.

"These kids are so young, all they've known is their daddy has been at war, their momma has been at war," says Allison Dickens, a guidance counselor at Highland Elementary School in Sanford, N.C., near Fort Bragg. "It's almost as if they don't have a normal childhood to compare it to."

War is . . . dangerous. And schools know that they need to prepare for the worst that could happen. "As a school, the best thing we could ever do is provide normalcy," says George Marston, principal of Rockfish Hoke Elementary, where 75% of 540 students have parents in the military. The Pentagon hires psychologists and social workers to work at military installations as "family life" consultants. Child care services also are offered. Community service groups, Boys and Girls Clubs of America, 4-H, chambers of commerce and veterans' organizations are enlisted by military family officials to assist children, particularly those of National Guard and Reserve families who live far from base support.

When the puppet show ended at Bill Hefner school, 7-year-old Meghan Dorr walked to the front of the multipurpose room to read remarks she'd prepared. She told classmates that her mother, a soldier in the Army, had returned from Iraq after a year away. "Don't feel sad, because your parents will come home," she reassured her classmates. "Just be brave and try your best in school and try to be strong."

—Gregg Zoroya

Five years after her dad came back from Vietnam, the family moved to Brussels, Belgium. In Europe Suzanne's father had even more opportunities for teaching his kids about battles and wars. A field of poppy flowers near their home turned into a lesson about the brutality of World War I

USA TODAY Snapshots®

Missing Americans

Servicemembers still listed as missing in action from these wars:

World War II	**73,690**
Korean War	**7,980**
Vietnam War	**1,681**
Gulf War	**2**
Iraq War	**1**
Afghanistan	**1**

Note: As of Nov. 8, 2011
Source: Defense Prisoner of War/Missing Personnel Office

By Anne R. Carey and Karl Gelles, USA TODAY, 2011

(1914–1918), in which her grandfather had been a soldier. This war was fought all across western Europe. It is still known for the horrors

Living abroad: The Collins family moved to Brussels, Belgium *(the city's Grand Place shown above)*, when Suzanne was school age. The family moved a lot because her dad was in the military.

Real-life history lessons: Collins's father took every opportunity to teach his family about military history. When they lived in Belgium, Collins's father would turn family outings, such as to a castle near Brussels, into military history lessons.

of its trench warfare and lethal chemical weapons. A trip to a castle, which Suzanne imagined would be as magical as a fairy tale, turned into a lesson about historical military fortresses. Her dad showed her arrow slits in the walls and the places where the castle's medieval defenders would have poured boiling oil on their enemies. It wasn't what Suzanne had in mind at all.

Suzanne's father also taught her about hunting and finding food in the wilderness. He had grown up during the Great Depression (1929–1942). It was a time when many Americans were unemployed and families did not have a lot of money. His family, for example, hunted as a way to put meat on the table. For them it was not a sport. He also learned about which plants in nature were edible. Suzanne remembers that he would bring home wild mushrooms and cook them. Her mother wouldn't let any of the kids eat them, fearing they were poisonous. But they never harmed her father, because he knew which ones were safe to eat and which ones were not.

The Great Depression

In 1929 the United States saw the end of decades of prosperity when the stock market crashed. Millions of people lost money they had invested in stocks. Banks also failed. Many people became bankrupt, and many industries and businesses also closed or laid off employees, leaving millions of people without jobs. Lack of consumer spending also forced other businesses to close. In addition to these financial problems, unusually dry weather in the American West destroyed many farms. Farmers without crops to sell to support their families lost their farms. Many of these unemployed and homeless people became migrants, traveling from place to place in broken-down vehicles, looking for work.

U.S. president Franklin D. Roosevelt developed a series of New Deal programs to help get the economy back on track and to create new jobs. All the same, the Depression held on until the United States joined the fighting forces of World War II (1939–1945) in 1941. Then U.S. industries kicked into high gear to manufacture tanks, airplanes, and other military equipment. These industries put many Americans back to work, and the Depression ended.

Hard times: Men wait in a line for free bread in New York City in February 1932. During the Great Depression, many Americans were out of work. To feed their families, many people waited in line for food donations.

Building a Life

After she graduated from high school in 1980, Suzanne decided to go to college at the Alabama School of Fine Arts. She also met an actor named Cap Pryor. They were married and moved to New York City. Suzanne decided to go to graduate school at New York University. She earned a master of fine arts degree in dramatic writing. Cap acted in several television series as well as in stage productions. Eventually she and Cap had two children, Charlie and Isabel.

After graduating from New York University, Collins got a job working for the children's television network Nickelodeon. She started writing

Cap and Suzanne: Collins met her future husband, Cap Pryor, when both attended the Alabama School of Fine Arts after high school. They are shown here in 2010, at an event celebrating *Time* magazine's 100 most influential people in the world, of which Collins was one.

scripts for several of Nickelodeon's shows, including *Clarissa Explains It All* (which was nominated for an Emmy award in 1994), *The Mystery Files of Shelby Woo*, and *Little Bear*. Eventually she became the head writer for the Scholastic Entertainment cartoon *Clifford's Puppy Days*, based on the antics of a popular character named *Clifford the Big Red Dog*.

USA TODAY
Life
SECTION D
LIFE.USATODAY.COM

THE HUNGER GAMES

CATCHING FIRE

MOCKINGJAY
SUZANNE COLLINS

April 28, 2003

Clifford woofs up success;
The Big Red Dog boosts Scholastic's green bottom line

<u>From the Pages of USA TODAY</u>

Even at age 40—in people years—Clifford the Big Red Dog seems to be increasingly wagging the tail at Scholastic Books. Here's what's on tap for Clifford:

- More TV. *Clifford's Puppy Days* hits PBS airwaves in September, after the wild success of the TV show *Clifford the Big Red Dog*. It introduces a new cast of characters and provides Scholastic with more licensing, toy and apparel opportunities.

- More books. Clifford is one of 10 characters featured in Fisher-Price's biggest initiative this year: Power Touch. The touch-and-read books teach phonics and reading with the touch of a finger. Clifford will be in stores in August.

- More big screen. A feature-length animated movie, expected to hit theaters in spring 2004, is in the works.

Clifford has 100 million books in print worldwide and is the top-ranked kids show for preschoolers. The show has four Daytime Emmy nominations this year, including one for Outstanding Children's Animated Program. The TV show promotes 10 Big Ideas such as "be kind" and "believe in yourself," while the book tells the story of Emily Elizabeth's unconditional love for the big red dog.

Puppy pal: Collins was head writer for the Scholastic Entertainment cartoon *Clifford's Puppy Days*. The show followed the puppy adventures of popular character Clifford the Big Red Dog and his owner, Emily Elizabeth.

The dog got its start in 1963 with the first Clifford book by Norman Bridwell. Scholastic doesn't expect Clifford's appeal to wane. "He's just big and red and fun," says Leslye Schaefer, senior vice president of marketing and consumer products for Scholastic Entertainment.

—Theresa Howard

***Santa, Baby!*:** Collins cowrote the animated holiday special *Santa, Baby!*, which aired on the Fox channel in 2001. The show was based on the popular Christmas song of the same name and featured the voices of Eartha Kitt and Gregory Hines.

Writing for children's television wasn't really so different from the kind of writing she would do later with the Hunger Games series. "Whatever age you're writing for, the same rules of plot, character, and theme apply. You just set up a world and try to remain true to it."

Suzanne also wrote several children's books, including *Fire Proof (Mystery Files of Shelby Woo, No. 11)*, based on some of the television shows for which she wrote. In 2001 she received a Writers Guild of America award in animation for cowriting the Christmas special *Santa, Baby!*

As Collins's children grew, she and her husband decided that they would leave New York City for a bigger home in Connecticut. And while Suzanne would continue to write scripts for children's television shows, she would soon find herself writing something completely different.

Writing for TV

A television show for children starts with a concept or idea. It might be a brand-new character and story, or it might be a character from an existing book. Once the basic idea is in place, writers develop characters. Most stories have four central characters: the hero, the antihero (villain), the love interest (children's shows don't often have this character), and the buddy. Then the writers must come up with a plotline, the story that gives the characters something to do and makes people want to watch them. Each episode of the show has a conflict or problem that is solved during the episode.

The script for a show is usually written by a group of writers who work together brainstorming the script and the specific lines the characters speak. Once they write the script, they create a storyboard. It shows each scene in the show. This is especially important for animated shows, where the animators need to know exactly what to draw. Actors are hired to play the characters or to provide their voices. In the final editing for an animated show, the animation and sounds are put together. A single half-hour episode of a children's animated television show will take about four weeks to write and six months to fully produce.

TV writing: Collins wrote for the Nickelodeon show *Clarissa Explains It All* in the 1990s, starring Melissa Joan Hart *(above)* as Clarissa.

Country living: Collins and her family moved to Connecticut from New York City in the early 2000s. She still worked as a screenwriter for children's television programs.

Gregor the Overlander

In 2003 Suzanne Collins was still writing television screenplays for Nickelodeon and other children's channels. While working on *Generation O!*—a television show for the Kids WB channel—she met a fellow television writer named James Proimos. Proimos wasn't just a screenwriter. He also wrote children's books such as *Paulie Pastrami Achieves World Peace* and *Todd's TV*.

Proimos and Collins became friends, and he began urging her to try her hand at writing a children's book. Proimos later recalled, "She seemed like a book writer to me; it was sort of her personality. She also had the style and the mind of a novelist. I was telling her that you can't do TV forever; it's a young person's business. With books, at the very worst, you start out slow, but you can do them for the rest of your life."

Intrigued by the idea, Suzanne began thinking about story ideas. One day she was thinking about the classic children's book *Alice's Adventures in Wonderland* and how the lovely countryside setting of that book would seem very strange to a kid who lived in an urban

Through the looking glass: The children's book *Alice's Adventures in Wonderland,* written in 1865 by British author Lewis Carroll, heavily influenced Collins's first foray into book writing.

place like New York City. Suzanne realized that in the city, a person would be more likely to fall down a manhole than a rabbit hole, as Alice does. And she also realized that in the city, a person wouldn't be very likely to find a tea party at the bottom of a manhole. This bit of thinking gave her the idea for what would become her first original children's book, *Gregor the Overlander*.

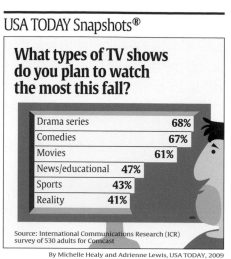

USA TODAY Snapshots®

What types of TV shows do you plan to watch the most this fall?

Drama series	68%
Comedies	67%
Movies	61%
News/educational	47%
Sports	43%
Reality	41%

Source: International Communications Research (ICR) survey of 530 adults for Comcast

By Michelle Healy and Adrienne Lewis, USA TODAY, 2009

A Ticket to Another World

Gregor the Overlander was the first book in what became a five-book series. Published in 2003, it is the story of an eleven-year-old boy named Gregor who is stuck at home for the summer with his two-year-old sister and his grandmother. His mother works, and his father has disappeared mysteriously several years before. Gregor and his sister, Boots, fall through a grate in the floor of their New York City apartment house. They find themselves in the Underland, where giant spiders, rats, and cockroaches live alongside humans. Collins has said of the Underland:

> I liked the fact that this world was teeming under New York City and nobody was aware of it. That you could be going along preoccupied with your own problems and then whoosh! You take a wrong turn in your laundry room and suddenly a giant cockroach is right in your face. No magic, no space or time travel, there's just a ticket to another world behind your clothes dryer.

A big city: New York City *(above)* is the setting for Collins's book *Gregor the Overlander.* It seems appropriate for a real-life city teeming with life to have inspired a story about an underworld just as busy.

Gregor is told that a prophecy predicts that an Overlander like him will play an important part in the future of the Underland. The threat of war hangs over the Underland. Gregor also discovers that the Underland might have something to do with his father's disappearance. Gregor and his sister, Boots, reluctantly go on a quest to rescue an Overlander prisoner who might just be their father. Members of all the different groups in the Underland help Gregor and Boots on the quest. The siblings find their father, who is sick but alive. They kill the rat king, who has threatened the Underland. Gregor, Boots, and their father return to New York City. At the end of the book, readers are left with hints that Gregor's role in the Underland is not yet finished.

Suzanne found it surprisingly easy to write about an eleven-year-old boy. "I remember being eleven very clearly and I had a lot of

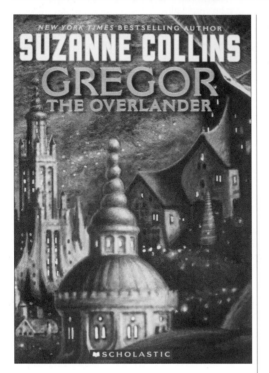

Gregor the Overlander: Collins published *Gregor the Overlander*, the first book in the Underland Chronicles series, in 2003. In all, there are five books in the series.

friends who were boys so it felt pretty natural being in Gregor's head," she said. She added, "I think I'm like Gregor because we both want to do the right thing but sometimes have trouble figuring out what it is. But Gregor is much braver than I am... if I even see a regular sized rat in New York City I immediately cross the street."

Gregor the Overlander is an adventure fantasy story, but Collins is aware that it is also a war story. The themes in the story are similar to those that would later emerge in the Hunger Games books. She commented, "Gregor falls into a fantastical world, but he's really acting out the main role in a war story. As the series continues, Gregor is faced with increasingly difficult quests and choices as the Underland breaks into a massive global war. His struggle to survive—both physically and spiritually—forms the arc of the The Underland Chronicles."

Gregor Meets the World

Gregor the Overlander received many positive reviews and awards. *Kirkus* reviewers said, "Gregor's luminous, supremely absorbing

USA TODAY

Life

SECTION D

LIFE.USATODAY.COM

February 9, 2012

At 50, 'A Wrinkle in Time' is still going strong

<u>From the Pages of USA TODAY</u>

It took Madeleine L'Engle two years to find a publisher for her 1962 novel, *A Wrinkle in Time*. Most editors feared the sci-fi/ fantasy about a young girl's quest to save her physicist dad from IT, a giant pulsating brain, would be too tough for kids. Librarians disagreed and awarded it the Newbery Medal. On the book's 50th anniversary, a look at the numbers:

<u>10 million</u>
Numbers of copies in print

<u>90th</u>
Ranking on the American Library Association's list of "most challenged" books (objections have ranged from L'Engle's "occultic worldview" to her overt Christianity)

<u>60</u>
Number of books written by L'Engle, who died in 2007 at 88

<u>26</u>
Rejection letters L'Engle received before her novel was bought by a friend of a friend, John Farrar of Farrar, Straus and Giroux

<u>1</u>
Copy sent into space in 1997 aboard the space shuttle *Endeavor* with astronaut Janice Voss, who says the novel sparked her interest in space when she was in sixth grade

<u>1</u>
Other Newbery Award-winning novel that's a homage to *A Wrinkle in Time*: Rebecca Stead's *When You Reach Me* (2009). Stead's main character reads *A Wrinkle in Time*.

—Bob Minzesheimer

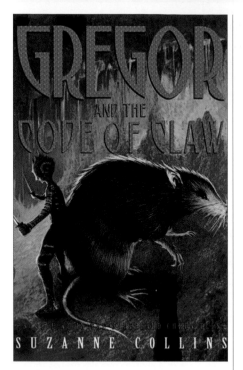

Underland Chronicles continue: Gregor has many adventures in the Underland. The final title in the series, *Gregor and the Code of Claw*, was published in 2007.

quest takes place in a strange underground land of giant cockroaches, rideable bats, and violet-eyed humans.... Creature depictions are soulful and the plot is riveting.... Wonderful."

After such positive reviews for this first book, Collins went on to write four more books in the Underland Chronicles series: *Gregor and the Prophecy of Bane* (2004), *Gregor and the Curse of the Warmbloods* (2005), *Gregor and the Marks of Secret* (2006), and *Gregor and the Code of Claw* (2007). These books follow Gregor's adventures as he returns to the Underland to slay an evil bat, goes on a quest to find a cure for a plague that infects his mother, fights against the rats again, and becomes involved in the prophecy where he must break a code so humanity can survive.

When asked about the violence in the Underland Chronicles series, Collins remarked, "Even though human characters die, a lot of the conflict takes place between different fantastical species. Giant rats and bats and things. If it's filled with cuddly animated animals, chances are no one's going to die. If it's filled with giant flesh-and-blood rats with a grudge, there's going to be violence." Readers and reviewers alike accepted the violence as part of Collins's worldview and praised the books. In fact, the entire Underland Chronicles series was listed as a *New York Times* best-selling series.

After Gregor

After completing the Underland Chronicles series, Collins went on to write a picture book for younger readers called *When Charlie McButton Lost Power*. It is the story of a little boy who doesn't know what to do with himself when a thunderstorm knocks out the power at his house.

Picture book: Collins published a picture book in 2005 called *When Charlie McButton Lost Power*.

Without his television and electronic games, he has to learn how to have fun playing with his sister.

But as *Charlie McButton* was hitting the bookstore shelves, Collins was already working on another book. It would explore some of the same themes as the Underland Chronicles series but for older readers. And it all started with an evening of channel surfing.

War zone: In 2007 a Black Hawk helicopter arrives to pick up soldiers after an operation in the U.S.-led war in Iraq. War takes its toll on lives at home and abroad—something Suzanne knows about firsthand.

Introducing Katniss

One night, Suzanne Collins was watching television, channel surfing with her remote in hand. She was flipping back and forth between a reality show and coverage of the U.S.-led war in Iraq (2003–2011). What she saw suddenly gave her the idea for the story that would become *The Hunger Games*:

I'm sitting there flipping around and on one channel there's a group of young people competing for, I don't know, money maybe? And on the next, there's a group of young people fighting an actual war. And I was tired, and the lines began to blur [between the reality show and the real-life war] in this very unsettling way, and I thought of this story.

Out of a few minutes of television, the story of Katniss Everdeen suddenly came to Collins. She would place her character in a futuristic world that drew heavily from both Greek mythology and Roman history.

Greek Inspiration

The story of *The Hunger Games*, the first of the Hunger Games trilogy, introduces readers to Katniss Everdeen and her world. Katniss herself is named for a type of edible water plant that Collins discovered in a book about surviving in the wild. It seemed like an excellent name for a girl who is forced by circumstance to find food for her family in the wild. She then has to use those same hunting and tracking skills to survive during the Hunger Games.

Katniss plant: This is one of a genus of edible water plants called *Sagittaria*, sometimes known as katniss. Thirty different varieties of *Sagittaria* are native to wetlands, primarily in the Americas.

IN FOCUS

Katniss

The katniss plant, after which the heroine of *The Hunger Games* is named, is also known as arrowhead, or Indian potato. It is a water plant with edible roots that taste a little like a sweet potato when they are cooked. Katniss is a very adaptable plant, able to withstand a wide range of temperatures. It can grow in many different types of soil.

However, the plot of *The Hunger Games* was also inspired by a classical Greek myth about Theseus and the Minotaur. Collins was very familiar with the Greek stories. "When I was a child, I was a fanatic about Greek mythology and this was one of my favorite myths," she said in an interview.

In this myth, powerful King Minos, who rules the isle of Crete, makes a deal with the citizens of the Greek city of Athens. He agrees not to attack Athens as long as the city sends seven Athenian boys and seven Athenian girls to Crete every year. There they are sent into a labyrinth (maze) from which it is impossible to escape and where they are devoured by a monster called the Minotaur.

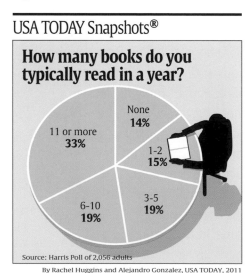

USA TODAY Snapshots®

How many books do you typically read in a year?

None 14%
11 or more 33%
1-2 15%
6-10 19%
3-5 19%

Source: Harris Poll of 2,056 adults

By Rachel Huggins and Alejandro Gonzalez, USA TODAY, 2011

Greek mythology: This Greek amphora (two-handled vase) dates to the 500s B.C. It depicts Theseus killing the Minotaur. Greek myths like this one sparked Collins's imagination as she was growing up.

Eventually Theseus, the son of the Athenian king, volunteers to go into the labyrinth. He kills the Minotaur and escapes from the maze. Collins explains, "Even when I was a little kid, this just stunned me because it was so cruel, the cruelest thing you could do to the people of Athens. Worse than killing them, he's killing their children."

Out of this myth came the idea for Katniss's story. She lives in a world called Panem. Like the people of Athens, the people in her district are forced by the government (the Capitol) to send a boy and a girl—called tributes—to the Hunger Games every year. And just as in the story of Theseus, the tributes are fighting to the death as they deal with the obstacles and traps set for them within the Hunger Games arena. Katniss survives the Games, just as Theseus survives the labyrinth. In fact, Collins says that Katniss is, in her own way, a futuristic Theseus.

IN F🞉CUS

The Hunger Games Trilogy: Cast of Characters

Katniss Everdeen: The narrator of all three books, Katniss is the main character and the female tribute from District 12. She survives the first Hunger Games and eventually becomes the Mockingjay, the symbol of the districts' rebellion.

Jennifer Lawrence

Peeta Mellark: Peeta is the male tribute from District 12. The son of a baker, he is in love with Katniss and will do anything he can to help her survive. Katniss must act as if she's in love with him to keep them both alive.

Josh Hutcherson

Gale Hawthorne: Also from District 12, Gale has been Katniss's friend since childhood. The two hunt together for food for their families in an area where the government

Liam Hemsworth

has made it illegal to go. Gale wants to start a rebellion to overthrow the government of Panem and ultimately works with the rebels.

Primrose Everdeen: Katniss's younger sister is sensitive and compassionate. She is a healer like her mother. Katniss takes Prim's place at the Hunger Games. Prim is killed in a bombing at the Capitol in the third book of the trilogy.

Mrs. Everdeen: Katniss and Prim's mother is a healer. She has suffered from depression ever since her husband, Katniss and Prim's father, was killed in a terrible mining accident.

Haymitch Abernathy: The only surviving District 12 winner of a past Hunger Games, Haymitch becomes the teacher and mentor of Katniss and Peeta as they prepare for the Games. He is also an alcoholic. He sends Katniss gifts during the Hunger Games to help her survive.

Woody Harrelson

Cinna: Katniss's stylist for the Hunger Games creates her costumes and becomes her friend. Later in the trilogy, he risks his life creating a wedding dress for Katniss that will transform into a Mockingjay outfit.

Lenny Kravitz

Rue: A tribute from District 11, Rue is small and quiet. She is very knowledgeable about nature and how to hide in the wilderness. She helps Katniss stay alive during the Games. When Rue is killed in the Games, Katniss sings to her, earning the support of Rue's district.

President Snow: The president of Panem forces Katniss to pretend to be in love with Peeta to keep her own family safe.

Plutarch Heavensbee: The head gamemaker for the 75th Hunger Games is secretly working with the rebels to overthrow the Capitol.

President Alma Coin: As president of District 13, she authorizes the bombing of the Capitol's children, which kills Katniss's sister, Prim. Katniss assassinates Coin.

Effie Trinket: Effie is the chaperone for District 12's tributes. She escorts them to the Capitol for the Games.

Elizabeth Banks

Roman Inspiration

Ancient history inspired another aspect of the *Hunger Games* story. In the days of the Roman Empire, gladiator games were an extremely popular form of public entertainment. In these games, trained gladiators (warriors)—each armed with specific, unique weapons—fought to the death in an open-air, public arena. These gladiators were the movie stars of their times. Successful gladiators could become rich and famous. If they lived long enough, they would eventually retire and train other gladiators.

Gladiators came from many different walks of life. Some who fought in gladiator games were condemned prisoners, slaves, or criminals who had been chosen to compete in the games. They had no choice but to fight. Other gladiators were free men who chose to participate just for the fortune and fame—and because they enjoyed it. Collins used three main elements of historic gladiator games in *The Hunger Games*: a ruthless government that sponsors ritualized violence, people who are forced to fight to the death, and the Games as a form of popular entertainment.

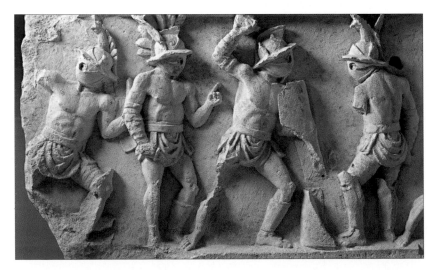

Gladiator games: This ancient Roman relief sculpture from the first century A.D. shows gladiators in battle. Citizens from Rome would gather to watch gladiators fight to the death. The winner of the match lived to fight another day.

USA TODAY
Life
SECTION D
LIFE.USATODAY.COM

July 25, 2002

Classics on odyssey from stuffy to cool; It's all Greek (and Latin) in popular lit classrooms

<u>From the Pages of USA TODAY</u> [There is a new] genuine interest in the ancient worlds of Greece and Rome. Bookstores groan with classical titles. Interest is particularly strong among the young. "There has been a resurgence [growth of new interest]," says assistant classics professor Mark Usher, 36. His students at the University of Vermont tell him, "I had no idea the Romans were so cool or the Greeks were so weird."

On TV, on the battlefield, this hunger for the classics extends beyond the page:

- High school enrollment in Latin classes is booming. The number of students taking the National Latin Exam has more than doubled since 1985 from 53,000 in 1985 to 123,000 in 2002. And more college students are choosing to major in the classics (Latin, Greek and classical civilization).
- Programs about the classical worlds of Rome and Greece always have been popular. Tales of antiquity [ancient times] draw a younger crowd than, say, the Civil War [1861–1865] or World War II.
- American Roman battle re-enactors forge their own helmets, carry shields and re-create the warfare of the Caesars [rulers of ancient Rome].

For the younger set, it doesn't hurt that J. K. Rowling laces her Harry Potter series with Latin phrases, spells and curses. There are plans to translate Rowling's books into Latin and ancient Greek. The appeal, however, is not just verb tenses and high SATs. Centuries later, the human drama of savage combat and warrior courage inspires still.

"I just think these are the greatest human-interest stories that have ever been told," author Michael Ford says. "They resonate just as much today as two millennia [thousand years] ago."

—Deirdre Donahue

In combining the Roman gladiator games with the Theseus myth, Collins says:

> In keeping with the classical roots, I send my tributes into an updated version of the Roman gladiator games, which [involves] a ruthless government forcing people to fight to the death as popular entertainment. The world of Panem, particularly the Capitol, is loaded with Roman references. Panem itself comes from the [Latin, the language of the ancient Romans] expression "Panem et Circenses," which translates into "Bread and Circuses."

In Roman times, "bread and circuses" were said to be the only two things necessary to keep the public happy and to allow politicians to rise to power: cheap food to eat and entertainment.

The idea for televising the Hunger Games all over Panem also draws its inspiration from both ancient Rome and modern reality television. In both cases, the audience plays a key role in the competition. The audience decides whether a participant wins or loses. For example, in *The Hunger Games*, the audience can send items such as food, water, and equipment to the contestants in the arena to help them survive. In Roman times, citizens at the games would show their approval for certain gladiators, often influencing an emperor's decision to allow the contestant to live or die. In modern times, reality show audiences can vote contestants on or off the show. Collins says of reality shows:

> Well, they're often set up as games and, like sporting events, there's an interest in seeing who wins. The contestants are usually unknown, which makes them relatable. Sometimes they have very talented people performing. Then there's the voyeuristic thrill—watching people being humiliated, or brought to tears, or suffering physically—which I find very disturbing.

1984

Suzanne Collins lists George Orwell's classic book *1984* as one of the books she loves and that she reads again and again. *The Hunger Games* and *1984* have similar themes. Published in 1949, *1984* is set in the future in a world where public mind control and surveillance are used to eliminate individuality.

Ahead of his time: George Orwell wrote *1984*, which was published in 1949.

The main character, Winston, falls in love with Julia. They both try to escape the control of Big Brother and the Party (the controlling power of their society). By the end of the book, both characters have been arrested and tortured and no longer love each other. Facing his execution, Winston realizes that he loves Big Brother and that the cultural brainwashing he had resisted before has succeeded with him.

The book *1984* is about a world similar to Panem, with two main characters who are independent thinkers and rebels. But in *The Hunger Games*, Katniss and Peeta are successful rebels. Some critics think that *The Hunger Games* is slightly more optimistic because American authors tend to be more hopeful about rebellions. British writers, like George Orwell, tend to be less optimistic.

There's also the potential for desensitizing the audience, so that when they see real tragedy playing out on, say, the news, it doesn't have the impact it should.

Reality bites: In the reality TV show *Survivor*, contestants compete in a variety of games to be the last survivor in the game. In a similar way, participants of the Hunger Games compete to be the last standing. However, Katniss and her fellow contestants are not volunteers. And those who lose pay with their own lives.

A Father's Inspiration

Beyond the influence of Greek mythology and Roman history, Collins also used her father's experiences as a child and as a soldier in Vietnam as she wrote *The Hunger Games*. His lessons about how to hunt and find edible plants, as well as his lessons about military tactics and weapons, helped her to construct the realistic world of Panem and the Games. Collins also read many books on wilderness survival. All these elements came together in Katniss's story, her life before the Reaping (where tributes are selected), her survival during the Games, and the struggle to remain herself once the Games are over and she—like a gladiator—has become a celebrity. As Katniss herself says at the end of the first book, "I stare in the mirror as I try to remember who I am and who I am not."

When *The Hunger Games* was published in 2008, Collins could not have known that she, too, was on the path to celebrity. Like Katniss, she would have to learn to deal with sudden fame.

District 12

Many avid readers of *The Hunger Games* feel that Katniss's District 12 is a futuristic version of the Appalachian region of the United States. Appalachia is a mountainous region of the eastern United States that is known for coal mining. Many areas of Appalachia are poverty stricken.

Like many of the tragic explosions that have occurred in Appalachian coal mines, a similar accident kills Katniss's father. In the second book of the Hunger Games trilogy, *Catching Fire*, the coal mines in District 12 are shut down for two weeks to punish the people there. Without money from their jobs, families are left to starve. This is a situation that is very similar to the strikes and conflicts between workers and managers of coal mines that took place in Appalachia during the twentieth century. Additionally, the knowledge that Katniss's mother and sister have about the natural healing power of plants is similar to the folk medicine that is still practiced in rural parts of Appalachia.

Coal mines: These men are coal miners, just like Katniss's father in *The Hunger Games*. This photograph was taken in the early 1900s. Coal mining is still a dangerous job.

CHAPTER FOUR

A big hit: *The Hunger Games* was published in October 2008. Little did Collins know at the time what a critical and popular success her book would become. In addition to being optioned for a movie series, it went on to earn several awards and honors and sell millions of copies in hard cover, paperback, and e-reader formats.

War Stories for Kids

■■■■■

The Hunger Games was published in October 2008. Critics almost immediately began to praise the book. Best-selling author Stephen King said:

> [*The Hunger Games*] is a violent, jarring, speed-rap of a novel that generates nearly constant suspense.... I couldn't stop reading.... Collins is an efficient

Early reviews: Hugely popular U.S. authors Stephen King *(left)* and Stephenie Meyer *(right)* were among the early reviewers of *The Hunger Games*. They both loved Collins's work.

no-nonsense prose stylist with a pleasantly dry sense of humor. [S]ince this is the first novel of a proposed trilogy, it seems to be that the essential question is whether or not readers will care enough to stick around and find out what comes next for Katniss. I know I will.

Stephenie Meyer, author of the hit Twilight series, said, "I was so obsessed with this book I had to take it with me out to dinner and hide it under the edge of the table so I wouldn't have to stop reading. The story kept me up for several nights in a row, because even after I was finished, I just lay in bed wide awake thinking about it. . . . *The Hunger Games* is amazing."

It was clear, especially as word of the book spread among both teen and adult readers, that Suzanne Collins was attracting a serious and loyal following. Her book was going to take its place alongside the Harry Potter and Twilight series. By the end of its first year, *The Hunger*

Games has been listed on the best-seller lists of the *New York Times, USA Today,* and *Publishers Weekly.* It was also named a 2008 Notable Book by *School Library Journal, The Horn Book, Booklist,* and the *New York Times.*

Exploring Themes

Almost as soon as *The Hunger Games* was published, reviewers began exploring its themes and messages. The book itself is a commentary on the horrors of war. Collins says she feels that young people need to be educated about war. At a young age, she herself had learned about the harsh realities of war from her father and his experiences in Vietnam. As an adult, she was disturbed by television coverage of the war in Iraq. She wanted to find a way to make the experience of war personal for young people. She also wanted to show young readers that through television, they were becoming desensitized to war and to violence. In the same way, she felt they were becoming desensitized to other human experiences through televised reality shows. "If we wait too long," Collins said of educating young readers about war, "what kind of expectation can we have [about kids understanding war]? We think we're sheltering them [from violence and harsh realities], but what we're doing is putting them at a disadvantage." She added, "If you're going to choose to do this topic, then you do it; if you say it's about these kids fighting to the death, then a lot of them have to die."

Collins was surprised at the variety of reader responses to the book. Some honed in on specific messages and themes, including romance. Some readers simply took the story at face value, viewing it as a story about teens and celebrity. Others noted the book's themes of severe poverty, starvation, and government oppression. Because the book came out at a time when the world's economy was beginning to take a downturn, some readers noted that Panem was a civilization of consumers and excessive spending. They felt that the book offered a sobering look at what the future of the United States might be.

Just How Low Can Reality Shows Go?

From the Pages of
USA TODAY

Reality TV has exploded. From MTV's *Real World* to NBC's *The Apprentice*, shows appear on just about every channel. So what's behind the craze? Once the laughed-at cheap and cheesy new kid on the block, reality TV now accounts for most successful new shows—so it's being taken much more seriously in the industry. It's less expensive than scripted shows to produce and although it doesn't have the syndication [repeat] life of a scripted show, several reality programs have had successful DVD sales.

Reality shows often concoct situations and instigate [set up] conflicts for dramatic effect. Then they edit down hundreds of hours of footage into about 44 minutes for an hour show. How fair is the finished product? Says Kimmi Kappenberg, *Australian Outback Survivor* contestant, "Everything that you saw us do or say, we did do or say. However, that is not the only thing we might have done or said."

So how low can these reality shows go? From *The Swan*, with women undergoing multiple plastic surgeries to compete in a beauty pageant, to *The WB's Superstar USA*, in which bad singers are told they're good only to humiliate them, reality shows seem to be finding new ways to low-ball the nation's taste. So just how low can they go? Says Mike Fleiss, creator of *Superstar* and *The Bachelor*, there's one definite prohibition: "No violence." But the Parents Television Council says reality TV is getting ever coarser. In a study released this week, the decency watchdog group looked at the first four episodes of 29 network reality series broadcast from June 2002 to August 2003. In 114.5 hours of programming, it found 1,135 instances of foul language; 492 instances of sexual content—either a verbal reference or visual act; and 30 instances of violence (fighting or wounds shown).

So why do we watch these things, even ones we denounce? "All of us are voyeurs [watchers]," says Paul Levinson, chairman of the department of communications and media studies at Fordham University [in New York]. "It's hard-wired into our being. If anything, it's amazing that reality TV didn't catch on faster than it did. It's such a natural," he says, adding, "Shakespeare said all the world's a stage. The greatest drama is what's really happening."

—Ann Oldenburg

Some parents and teachers have said the book is a good way to get teens to talk about their own struggles, especially their struggles with popularity. Being popular—and not being popular—can be difficult for teens to manage. But Collins has held firm to the belief that her book is about educating kids about what war really is. "I don't write about adolescents. I write about war, for adolescents," she insists.

The Critics

Not everyone loves *The Hunger Games*. Some critics have said that the writing is not especially good. Others have said that Collins spends too much time describing small things such as clothing and food, even when she claims that these things are not important. Others have objected to the violence in the story. A parent in Goffstown, New Hampshire, asked her school board to ban the book from her daughter's seventh-grade classroom. The parent claimed that the book contained too much violence and gave her daughter nightmares. (The parent had not actually read the book.)

Another reader, who reviews books on her blog, disliked the book for many reasons. She wrote:

Certainly, it was a gripping read, and Katniss and Peeta are heroes working against the norm of Panem. But I was still watching a horrible display of survival skills in which teenagers, mostly rotten ones, are killing each other. I hated it. I didn't like the writing (present tense, which at times seemed invisible and at other times jarring). I didn't like the romance element (Katniss pretends to be in love in order to win). I didn't like the ignorance (Katniss is ignorant that Peeta loves her; Katniss is ignorant of the danger of rejecting the Capitol, which seemed to take away from the power of her defiance). I just plain didn't like it.

December 28, 1999

Popularity of 'Potter' stirs cauldron of dissent, books' foes cite rights of parents, free speech

<u>From the Pages of USA TODAY</u>

[*The Hunger Games* is certainly not the first book that parents have asked to be banned from classrooms. The Harry Potter books have had their share of controversy, too.] In a dozen school systems in eight states from New York to California, J. K. Rowling's three tales starring famous child wizard Harry Potter have sparked controversy, not magic, as parents and others brand Harry a handbook for witchcraft and violence.

And those are only the verified cases. The American Library Association (ALA) estimates that for every public book challenge, there are four or five others bubbling under the surface. That means every week, if not every day, some book, whether *Huckleberry Finn* or *Harry Potter and the Sorcerer's Stone*, is discreetly removed from the classroom or pulled from the library shelves, according to the ALA. Though nationally the Harry Potter dispute isn't as aggressive and systematic as past book conflicts, it represents another in a long line of battles that have weighed the sensibilities of students and parents against constitutional protections of free speech.

Last year, 500 reports of challenges to novels and textbooks poured into the ALA's office of intellectual freedom in Chicago—51 from Texas alone. Though Judith Krug, the office's director, says the numbers have held steady the past few years, she has a feeling "a lot more is going on." Challenges to Harry Potter-type book series are recorded as only one incident, even though each series may contain up to 15 volumes.

Harry Potter critics say their cause is less about abridging a teacher's right to teach a particular book and more about a parent's right to shape a child's curriculum, whether in English class or sex ed. "This is not an issue of good book vs. bad book," says Karen Jo Gounaud, president of Family Friendly Libraries. "This is a question of appropriateness, and undermining parental authority is something to be concerned about."

(continued on next page)

Experts say that by promoting vigorous debate, book challenges are an integral part of American intellectual values. The First Amendment [of the Constitution] protects speech, particularly unpopular speech. In the case of Harry Potter, says Don Dingledine, an English professor at Temple University in Philadelphia [Pennsylvania] who teaches a course on banned books, the experts note that complaints are bipartisan, historically coming from the left and the right . . . from urban and rural areas. "I'm hoping teachers will bring the controversy into the classroom," Dingledine says. "What better way to train students to have critical thinking skills?"

Gounaud knows a parent who was told by a teacher, "I don't want your child saying negative things about Harry Potter in class. She should keep her opinions to herself." The principal resolved the situation, Gounaud says, allowing the girl to voice her opinion "as long as it's not disruptive. This gets down to the nitty-gritty of a child's own right to freedom of speech," she says.

But Krug thinks parents who try to control what their kids read are disingenuous [using a false argument] to argue free speech. "I don't see all these complaints to be of concern to a child at all," she says. "Parents are concerned their child will have a unique thought . . . or will start exploring areas parents don't want them to explore."

Gounaud says her phone rang non-stop recently with Harry Potter concerns, some from Christian teachers who feel pressured to read something they find anti-Christian. . . . [Yet] Chuck Colson, a Christian broadcaster . . . calls Harry Potter "enormously inventive," reassuring anxious parents that the magic is "mechanical, as opposed to occultic [evil]." As Harry and his friends struggle between good and evil, "they don't make contact with a supernatural world."

Sharon Newman, who directs a youth ministry at a Lansing, N.Y., church, plans to approach her local school superintendent about getting equal time in the classroom: If Harry Potter's brand of witchcraft gets attention, so should Christianity (and Judaism and Islam). Newman, who has no children, says she knows a handful of worried parents who keep quiet.

When a parent limits a child's reading choices, that's fine, says Elliot Mincberg of People for the American Way. When a parent tries to limit other children's choices, that's "deplorable. These tend to be books that excite a child's imagination. But that's what children's literature has been about for hundreds of years, whether *Grimm's Fairy Tales* or *The Wizard of Oz*."

The controversy has spurred thorny he-said/she-said debates between parents and educators. In Citrus Heights, Calif., Kim Reckers walked into the principal's office at her son's school after Garth, 9, came home and said his teacher had shared bits of *Harry Potter* with the class and recommended that students read it. "I didn't want this book read to any of the children in the whole school," says Reckers, a Christian. "It's a really bad book," replete with [full of] darkness and death. "I can't believe people have given this awards. It's sad. It's scary, actually."

Joyce Nein, principal of Carriage Drive Elementary, denies that *Harry Potter* was read to the class and can't confirm that the teacher recommended it. Nein says Reckers is the only parent to complain in a school with 600 pupils. The teacher refused to comment.

Reckers says she has "never, ever" prevented her kids from reading a book and says she is not "fanatical." But "kids get so into this book, they feel they're a part of what's going on. With *The Wizard of Oz*, kids know that's more pretend." Garth, who says he's OK with his mother's decision, has a handful of friends who are reading *Harry Potter*. "I don't know if they really like it," the fourth-grader says. "They're probably reading it because they heard from their teacher it's real good, stuff like that."

In the Rockwood [Missouri] School District in St. Louis, *Harry Potter* is not on the curriculum but is in the library and, says Tamara Rhomberg, language arts coordinator for kindergarten through fifth grade, on about half the student desks. Some teachers are reading it aloud, but any student can bring it for silent reading periods. In some classrooms, the books become the grade-school equivalent of sneaking a cigarette.

Historically, challenging books has proved a sure-fire way to spike their popularity. A generation ago, well-thumbed and underlined copies of *The Catcher in the Rye* were passed around among adolescents. Temple University professor Don Dingledine lovingly recalls stealing away to a "dark corner of the library" as a teenager to sneak a glance at *Forever*, Judy Blume's 1975 sexually explicit coming-of-age classic. "The freedom to choose individual books, that's a powerful tool for a class," Dingledine says, "and that's exactly what would-be censors are trying to take away from us."

—Olivia Barker

In addition, many reviewers pointed out the plot similarity between *The Hunger Games* and a Japanese novel published in 1999 called *Battle Royale*. Some even called *The Hunger Games* a rip-off of that earlier book. However, Collins has said that she'd never even heard of the book before *The Hunger Games* was published.

Attracting a Following

Teachers and librarians were also noticing that *The Hunger Games* attracted kids—especially boys—who don't usually like to read. Because the book is fast-paced and keeps readers reading to see what will happen next, it is a great way to get the attention of kids who usually don't make time to read books. And because the book does not focus only on romance—as the Twilight series does—it appeals to boys as well as girls. Collins thinks this is because the story has a female lead character within a gladiator story. This type of story traditionally features a male lead character. Collins loves that the book is reaching out and appealing to kids who usually don't like to read.

Teen readers: Teen boys are among the many fans of the Hunger Games trilogy.

Battle Royale

Battle Royale is a Japanese dystopian novel written by Koushun Takami in 1999 and published in English in 2003. (Dystopian stories deal with societies in which people live in oppressive conditions with little freedom or happiness.) Many people have compared the plot of *The Hunger Games* to *Battle Royale* because both books deal with young people who have to fight to the death. In *Battle Royale*, forty-two high school students are taken every year on what is supposed to be a field trip, only to find that they are part of something called the Program.

In the story, the Program was originally a military research project but has become a way of terrorizing and controlling the population. The students are taken to an island, given a random weapon (anything from a gun to a paper fan to a pot lid) and supplies, and then released on the island. They wear collars that will explode if they attempt to escape. Through various episodes of violence and trickery, one student is declared the winner. However, three students actually escape the island to the winner's boat. The book ends with the four students on their way to the United States and an uncertain future. *Battle Royale* was adapted into two movie and several manga (Japanese comics) editions.

Japanese Hunger Games: This is a still from the movie version of *Battle Royale*, based on a novel written by Japanese author Koushun Takami and published in 1999. Readers of both books see many similarities between *Battle Royale* and *The Hunger Games*.

One of the most memorable things I hear is when someone tells me that my books got a reluctant reader to read. They'll say, "You know, there's this kid and he wouldn't touch a book and his parents found him under a blanket with a flashlight after bedtime because he couldn't wait to find out what happened in the next chapter." That's just the best feeling. The idea that you might have contributed to a child's enjoyment of reading.

Because Collins had planned *The Hunger Games* as a trilogy from the start, readers were soon clamoring for the next book in the series. And after a relatively quiet release for *The Hunger Games*, the release of *Catching Fire*, the second book in the series, would be an entirely different experience.

USA TODAY Snapshots®

The nation's best sellers

Top five best sellers, shown in proportion of sales. Example: For every 10 copies of *The Help* sold, 1.6 copies of *The Hunger Games* were sold:

The Help
Kathryn Stockett — 10

The Hunger Games
Suzanne Collins — 1.6

Heaven Is for Real
Todd Burpo with Lynn Vincent — 1.5

Blind Faith
C.J. Lyons — 1.5

Catching Fire
Suzanne Collins — 1.1

Thursday: Top 50 books list (top150.usatoday.com)

Source: USA TODAY Best-Selling Books   USA TODAY, 2011

The next book: The story of Katniss and Peeta continues in Collins's second book, *Catching Fire* (2009).

Completing the Trilogy

The second book in the Hunger Games trilogy, *Catching Fire*, was originally planned for release on September 8, 2009. But retailers asked the book's publisher, Scholastic, to release it before Labor Day and before school started for most kids. They wanted kids to have the chance to buy and read the book before they had to focus on school and homework. The date was moved up to September 1.

The book, just like the first book in the series, was an immediate best seller.

Catching Fire continues the story of *The Hunger Games*. It starts just days after Katniss and Peeta have both been announced as the winners of the Hunger Games. Katniss and Peeta are set to return home to District 12, after a victory tour of all the districts. The president of Panem, President Snow, unexpectedly visits Katniss and informs her that her actions during the Hunger Games have led to a

Suzanne meets a fan: Shortly before the release of *Catching Fire,* Collins met with Kayley Hyde *(left),* winner of an essay contest put on by Suzanne's publisher. Participants answered this question in five hundred words or less: "How would you survive the Hunger Games?" As the winner, Kayley Hyde won a trip to New York City, lunch with the author, and signed copies of the first two installments of the Hunger Games trilogy.

rebellion among the districts. She is forced to pretend that her actions were motivated by her overwhelming love for Peeta and were not meant as an act of defiance. If she does not keep up the pretense of being in love with Peeta, President Snow tells her that her family will be in danger.

During the victory tour, Katniss and Peeta pretend to be in love (although Peeta really is in love with Katniss). Peeta proposes to Katniss on television to further the impression that they are a romantic couple. However, it is then decided that the next Hunger Games will actually be a Quarter Quell, when twenty-four past winners—including Peeta and Katniss—will be forced to compete again. The Quarter Quell Games end when several competitors break through the arena's force field. Katniss is knocked unconscious and awakens to find herself being transported out of the arena and toward the mysterious District 13, the center of the rebellion. Katniss learns that her own district, District 12, has been bombed but that her family escaped to safety.

Scholastic had also heightened the anticipation of the book by sponsoring a writing contest for young readers. The contest asked them to write about the question, "How would you survive the Hunger Games?" The winner was Kayley Hyde, a seventeen-year-old girl from the state of Washington. Her winning entry began like this:

> Words are powerful things. So often people throughout the world underestimate their infinite abilities. Words bring us together, tear us apart, create music and incite laughter. They can express emotion, tell it like it is and even save a life. So why couldn't they help me win the Hunger Games?

Kayley won a trip to New York to have a private lunch with Suzanne Collins. She also won a signed copy of *The Hunger Games* and a copy of *Catching Fire* before it was available to the general public.

USA TODAY
Life
SECTION D
LIFE.USATODAY.COM

September 1, 2009

Let the "Games" Continue

<u>From the Pages of USA TODAY</u>

Suzanne Collins [*below*], author of publishing's hottest new teen series, *The Hunger Games*, says the most common question readers ask isn't about its violence or political undercurrents, but its budding love story. *Catching Fire*, second in a trilogy, advances but doesn't resolve a romantic triangle angling its 16-year-old narrator between two jealous boyfriends. Love can wait, Collins says. "She's got a lot of things on her plate—like staying alive and saving humanity." Katniss cares about the two boys, but not in the same way they love her, Collins says. "She's not that interested in romance. She equates love with marriage and kids, who could be sent to the games."

Readers, however, are taken by Katniss's romantic prospects. The Internet is filled with debates about her best potential mate. If you search Google for Katniss Everdeen, you will get 50,300 results—just one year after she appeared in print.

In Croton-on-Hudson, N.Y., where *The Hunger Games* is among 49 books on the ninth-grade summer reading list (students chose three), teacher Annmarie Powers says her students introduced her to the series. It "spread like wildfire," she says, with themes that teens are consumed with: "fairness, relationships, plenty of violence and blood, greed, hypocrisy, subservience and rebellion."

—Bob Minzesheimer

Romance

As readers devoured *Catching Fire*, Collins was surprised to find that many of her readers were focusing on the love triangle of Katniss, Peeta, and Gale. Internet sites were even selling Team Peeta and Team Gale T-shirts. Collins said:

> Romance is very powerful. You have to be careful with it, because I know for myself, if there is a romance in something—even in an action movie, even if it's not very developed—I still want to see how it turns out. I just started out with it in the initial story, and the romance sort of naturally developed. Then it became far more key than I had anticipated, and the reason it did is that Peeta makes it a strategy in the game. Well, once [romance] is tied in to the game, the two become inseparable.

Planning a Trilogy

Because Collins had always planned to write a trilogy about Katniss and the Hunger Games, readers were impatient for the third and final book in the set. Collins said, "This one was always a trilogy. Every book is leading to the larger conclusion. I came from [a] theater [background], and the books are basically structured like three-act plays." *Catching Fire* was act 2 in Katniss's story. Even though Collins did not have every detail of every book planned before she started writing the first one, she knew the overall arc of the story. *Catching Fire* was part of that arc, which started with the gladiator-style game, moved on to a revolution, and then to a war and a conclusion. Collins has said the following about writing the series:

> I've learned it helps me to work out the key structural points before I begin a story. The inciting incident, acts, breaks, mid-story reversal, crisis, climax, those sorts of things. I'll know a lot of what fills the spaces between them as well, but I leave some uncharted room for the characters to develop. And if a

door opens along the way, and I'm intrigued by where it leads, I'll definitely go through it.

Collins has also commented that it was not especially difficult to write the two books after *The Hunger Games* because the production of all three volumes overlapped. Revising one book would overlap with writing the next book, and she felt as if she never left Panem until all three were completed.

Mockingjay

The third and final book in the Hunger Games trilogy, *Mockingjay*, was released on August 24, 2010. As with the release of the Harry Potter books and the Twilight books, this time, fans lined up outside bookstores to purchase copies as soon as the clock struck 12:01 A.M. on the release day. The book sold 450,000 copies in the first week, and the publisher quickly reprinted 400,000 more.

Mockingjay opens with Katniss agreeing to be the Mockingjay, the symbol of rebellion for Panem's districts. She helps to rescue Peeta and others who have been held captive in the Capitol. But she finds that Peeta has been brainwashed by the Capitol so that he now views all rebels as evil. He tries to kill her when they see each other again. When the district rebels begin to attack the Capitol, Katniss approaches the mansion of President Snow, whom she intends to kill.

Mockingjay: Collins finished the trilogy with a book called *Mockingjay*. It sold half a million copies in its first week.

Teen Alert: 'Mockingjay' Arrives Early Tuesday

From the Pages of USA TODAY

If more than the usual number of teens seem sleepy next Tuesday, blame (or credit) novelist Suzanne Collins. *Mockingjay*, the last in Collins's *Hunger Games* trilogy for teens, will be released at 12:01 A.M. Tuesday, triggering scores of midnight parties at bookstores. Not since *Harry Potter* and *Twilight* has a novel been expected to keep so many young readers (and some adults) up all night.

Collins's cliffhanging series (*The Hunger Games* and *Catching Fire* were the first two books), set in a future dictatorship that forces teenagers to fight to the death on TV, is the most popular example of a boom in dystopian novels, in which teens struggle to survive in nightmarish worlds.

Collins's popularity "is huge," says Shari Conradson, a teacher in Sebastopol, Calif. She's often asked by students for "other books like *The Hunger Games*." What's the appeal? Teens "recognize the issues in these books without having to face them dead-on," Conradson says. "In many of them, teen characters are the heroes and make the world a better place."

Kayley Hyde, 18, of Edmonds, Wash., who won a Hunger Games essay contest last year and lunch with Collins, says she loves "reading about what people think our country or our world could become."

Collins, who'll attend her first midnight release party at New York's Books of Wonder, hopes to keep *Mockingjay*'s plot a secret until Tuesday. She hopes kids where school has started won't stay home to read her book: "At the risk of sounding ungrateful, please go to school. So many kids in the world never get a chance to. That being said, if you wanted to stay up late reading, I wouldn't be the one taking the flashlight away from you."

—Bob Minzesheimer

Rebel children and medics—among them Katniss's sister, Prim—are gathered at the mansion, supposedly for their protection but actually to serve as a human shield for Snow. They are killed when bombs placed in supply packages go off.

Katniss is about to kill President Snow when she realizes that the plot that killed her own sister may have been created by her friend Gale and the leader of District 13, President Coin. Coin discusses starting a new version of the Hunger Games as a punishment for those who live in the Capitol district and never had to participate in the previous Hunger Games. Katniss, fearful that the leaders of the rebellion are simply replacing the Capitol government with an equally bad government, aims her killing shot at Coin instead of at President Snow. However, even though Katniss does not shoot him, Snow still dies in the same scene, apparently trampled by the crowd. Katniss is arrested for killing Coin but is acquitted on the grounds that she is insane. She returns home. Peeta, who has recovered from his brainwashing, also returns to District 12. The book ends fifteen years later, with Peeta and Katniss married and the parents of two children. Katniss fears the day when her children will learn about the roles their parents played in the Hunger Games. She worries about what they will think of their parents as a result. The trilogy concludes with no hint of more books in the series.

Not a Happy Ending

Many readers were disappointed that Katniss's story has so much tragedy and does not end on a happily-ever-after note. For example, when Collins's agent, Rosemary Stimola, first read the manuscript of *Mockingjay* and came to the part where Katniss's sister dies in the bombing, she called Collins and wailed, "No! Don't do it!" Even though the book was still at the stage where it could be changed, Collins refused to alter Prim's death. Collins told Stimola that the story had to be that way, because in war there are tragic losses that have to be mourned.

IN FOCUS

Controversial Endings?

Before J. K. Rowling published the final book in her Harry Potter series, controversy surrounded the question of whether her main character, Harry, would be killed at the end of the series. People who were familiar with other epic journey tales argued that most of the time, the main character dies after accomplishing the goal he or she has. Many people were afraid that killing off Harry would be depressing and heartbreaking for all Rowling's young readers. Ultimately, Rowling did not disappoint her fans, and Harry survived at the end of book 7 and seemed to go on to live a happy life.

Suzanne Collins, however, insists that her Hunger Games books are about war, and in war, people die. Katniss does survive, but she will never be the same again. And not only does her sister die, but so do other characters the reader has come to like, such as Cinna, other tributes from the Quarter Quell games, and many people from District 12.

In the epilogue of *Mockingjay*, an older and wiser Katniss makes a list in her head "of every act of goodness I've seen someone do. It's like a game. Repetitive. Even a little tedious. . . . But there are much worse games to play."

Harry Potter: Daniel Radcliffe plays Harry Potter, one of the most well-known characters from juvenile fiction of the twenty-first century. Here, Harry appears outside of Hogwarts Academy in a scene from the movie *Harry Potter and the Deathly Hallows: Part 2* (2011).

July 14, 2011

How Harry Potter Magically Changed Films

From the Pages of
USA TODAY
Who would have guessed a bespectacled boy wizard from the 'burbs of Britain could cast a spell powerful enough to radically change the way movies are made? The magical box-office reign of Harry Potter reached a thunderous climax when the final installment *Harry Potter and the Deathly Hallows, Part 2* opened. The previous seven movies based on J. K. Rowling's phenomenally successful books have grossed $6.4 billion, making Potter the most successful movie franchise in history. The stories have been ingrained in global popular culture, and the movies, which are almost as beloved as Rowling's best sellers (a rare phenomenon itself) will leave an indelible mark on cinema history. "If you had mentioned the name Harry Potter 13 years ago, people would have thought it was someone's accountant," says Potter screenwriter Steve Kloves. "Now you can go to Zimbabwe [in Africa] and everyone knows who that is."

The filmmakers had the challenging task of creating movies faithful to the beloved novels, yet distinctive. Chris Columbus directed the first two films, *Harry Potter and the Sorcerer's Stone* (2001) and *Harry Potter and the Chamber of Secrets* (2002). He had a definite idea in mind when laying the groundwork for the series, which has gone on to be helmed [led] by three other directors, most recently by David Yates, who directed the last four films.

Led initially perhaps by their children, but then entranced by Rowling's witty language and multi-layered characters, adults also embraced Potter books and attended the movies in droves. "There was a sea change with Harry Potter," says Erik Feig, president of worldwide production at Summit Entertainment, which has made the Twilight movies. "The story has a younger protagonist [lead character], but the book series and the movies are greatly enjoyed by older people, too. I devoured the first book and gave it to every grown-up I knew. We saw the same thing with *Twilight*. They drew all audiences. It was an inspiration to us."

"The impact of the Potter series has been tremendous in that it has essentially become the idea of a modern franchise," says director Chris Weitz (T*wilight: New Moon; The Golden Compass*). "They latched onto something that has its own sequels built in. Now everyone is looking for a literary property that extends enough for them to keep on building. "It's led to this speculative bubble in mystical young-adult fiction. *Twilight* found its own way to hit upon the hunger for the supernatural and a particular time of life. But if you look at the bookshelves now, half of what is coming out in young adult fiction is about a werewolf or a vampire or angels or demons. The other half is about magic and wizardry."

[Without] *Potter*, there probably would have been no *Twilight* blockbuster movies, and *Pirates of the Caribbean* might have been a one-time film. "Some of the effects of Potter are incredibly positive, and some are less so," says Daniel Radcliffe, 21, who plays Harry Potter. "The great thing is that it has proved that a big studio movie franchise can also have a huge amount of integrity. There are many examples of franchises that are just people cashing in, regardless of what the source material is. "The first *Matrix* was one of the best films of its decade. It was never designed to be a trilogy, but people saw dollar signs," Radcliffe says. "Personally, I think people get slightly irritated when a new *Pirates of the Caribbean* comes out. What about quitting when you're ahead? We have a huge amount of respect for our audience, and we have wonderful source material. It was never a sense of, 'Let's pad out this series to make money.'"

Thanks to *Potter*, voracious young readers of popular books may hold more sway in Hollywood than A-list actors. "I think people were hesitant to put a lot of faith in an audience of kids," Radcliffe says. "The tendency is to think kids have a very short attention span. But if you find something that can engage them, they are the most ferocious followers. Without the example of *Potter*, I don't think people would have believed they would have been able to maintain and sustain the interest of a young audience."

Now the focus is on Potter devotees [fans]. "We want to do right by all of the loyal and passionate fans," says Alli Shearmur, president of production at Lionsgate, which is adapting Suzanne Collins's *The Hunger Games*, scheduled for release in March of 2012. "We want to connect with fans directly and create opportunities for them to be part of the process."

—Claudia Puig

Like the first two books in the series, *Mockingjay* received many awards and was on the top of most best-seller lists. And while many readers hoped that perhaps Collins would change her mind and write more books in the series, she remains firm that there will only ever be these three. "I think a series should be absolutely as long as it takes you to tell your story," she says. "To arbitrarily go on and do books past the natural life of the story, I don't think you're doing the book or your audience a service."

Dealing with Fame

With the tremendous success of the Hunger Games trilogy, Suzanne Collins has had to deal with the extraordinary demands of fame. She has found herself facing the need to give interviews to magazines and newspapers; appear on television; travel on book tours; meet fans; and dodge unwanted attention from photographers and overeager fans who want autographs, photographs, and writing advice. But Collins is a very private person who wants to protect a quiet life for herself and her family. In addition, some of Collins's fans feel that it is clear from the Hunger Games trilogy that Collins views being a celebrity as an empty and dangerous role that harms individuals. For this reason, they see her reluctance to give interviews and to appear before cameras as ways to keep her exposure to harmful media to a minimum.

Fame at a price: Suzanne's hit series put her in the public eye in a way she neither expected nor wanted. Here she is at a book festival in Washington, D.C., in 2010.

All the same, Collins keeps a low profile without disappointing her fans. She has a very basic website, with information about her books, a few simple photographs, and a short interview with an editor from Scholastic Press. She does occasionally give interviews with print journals, such as the *New York Times* and *School Library Journal*, and also sometimes grants audio and video interviews and does readings at bookstores. Yet she does not allow videotaping at her public readings. And when she does do interviews, she often answers questions in a way that makes it seem as if she is reading from a prepared script. Collins seems to feel that her books speak for themselves, and her celebrity status as an author is not necessary. Readers will get to know her by reading her books.

The Hunger Games . . . on the Big Screen

All the same, the release of the final book in the Hunger Games series was only part of its popularity. Since the announcement in 2009 that Lionsgate had optioned *The Hunger Games* for a possible movie, fans had been wondering when the movie was actually going to be in the works. As 2010 drew to a close, they were about to get an answer.

On the big screen: Collins's book came to life on the movie screen in 2012. This is a still from *The Hunger Games* (movie), showing Jennifer Lawrence as Katniss.

The Big Screen

Fans of *The Hunger Games* have known since 2009 that the book had been optioned as a possible movie. Lionsgate had acquired worldwide distribution rights to make a movie from the book. But the question was when would it actually happen? And who would write the screenplay?

Book to Movie

In early 2010, Lionsgate and a company called Color Force began to adapt *The*

Hunger Games book into a movie. Suzanne Collins was asked to write the first draft of the script. She told an interviewer why she felt it was important for her to write that first draft:

> I was writing the third book and there was great secrecy about it and no one could know how it ended. But I knew that if the screenplay got off on the wrong foot, that you could end up with something by which you could never reach the events of the third book. And since I couldn't reveal information to the film team, I wanted to be around to keep an eye on that. After that, I didn't know.

For the next draft of the script, the movie company brought in Billy Ray, an experienced screenplay writer, to develop the script even further. Collins said of Billy Ray, "Amazingly talented, collaborative, and always respectful of the book, . . . [the adaptation would] further explore the world of Panem and its inhabitants."

Working with Gary Ross

Once a second draft had been finished, it went to Gary Ross, who would direct *The Hunger Games*. He is known as a director who needs to put his own voice

A collaboration: Collins and Billy Ray put their talents together to turn *The Hunger Games* into a screenplay for the movie.

A world premiere: Collins and *The Hunger Games* cowriter and director Gary Ross appear together at the world premiere of the movie in Los Angeles. Ross has written and directed several popular Hollywood movies. He earned an Oscar nomination for Best Original Screenplay for *Big* (1988), starring Tom Hanks. And he wrote the screenplay for the film version of the Newbery Award–winning children's book *The Tale of Despereaux* (2003) by Kate DiCamillo.

in a script. This means that he wants to see the story through his own eyes as well as the way it was told in the book. So he and Collins got together and began to work on another draft of the script together. Collins, as a former television writer, was used to working in collaboration with other writers. She knew that it could take a little while to discover if she would "click" with another writer. To her delight, she and Ross found out that they were compatible almost right away. After a few minutes of discussion, they began writing together immediately. Ross said, "[Suzanne would] pitch a line and I'd pitch the next line and before you knew it, we had a dialogue scene. And then we were both just getting excited from that."

Writing a movie script from a book is difficult. A book often has to be shortened and condensed to fit into a two-hour movie. *The Hunger Games* book is also written in the present tense and from the first-person point of view. These literary techniques aren't easy to translate into the dramatic perspective of a movie, which typically works from a different point of view—the audience's.

Collins and Ross also had to think carefully about how to present the book's violence on the big screen. They wanted to maintain a PG-13 rating for the movie so that the book's young fans would be able to see it. Ross felt strongly that this was a story that belonged to teenagers. He felt they deserved to be able to access it completely. This meant changing some of the violence, since many things that are acceptable on a book page are not appropriate on the big screen.

Collins has said that after years of writing the Hunger Games books alone, she enjoyed being back in a situation where she was writing with another person. Ross also discovered that Collins's television background made her more knowledgeable about the filmmaking process than most writers. For this reason, she was able to discuss set and costume design as well as casting with Ross.

With the script finished, the movie was scheduled to begin production. A release date of March 23, 2012, was announced to the public. It was time to find actors to fill the roles.

USA TODAY Snapshots®

Some R-rated films okay for teens
R-rated movies parents would allow their teens to see:

When Harry Met Sally	**92%**
Schindler's List	**91%**
Saving Private Ryan	**91%**
Pretty Woman	**90%**
Alien	**90%**

Source: *Family Circle*   By Cindy Hall and Marcy E. Mullins, USA TODAY, 2001

PG-13 is secret to film success; Not too naughty, but not very nice

From the Pages of USA TODAY   A PG-13 rating is often the key to a movie's success. The major studios have found a secret to box office success: Avoid the G rating with a four-letter word or some sexual innuendo so that teens and pre-teens won't think you're putting out a "baby" movie. And avoid the R so theater managers won't catch heat for letting under-17s into R-rated films.

The PG rating appeals to movie-savvy teens who find a G rating too juvenile. PG-13 is even better, implying the movie goes about as far as it can without kids having to be taken by parents if they want to see it. "PG-13 is the commercial sweet spot, and that's what they're aiming for," says Nell Minow, author of *The Movie Mom's Guide to Family Movies.*

Movie industry honchos call this the triumph of the "family film." "Family product sells, and R-rated product does not," John Fithian, president of the National Association of Theatre Owners, says. But critics of the ratings system say that when you spice up G-rated material or slightly tone down R-rated content, what you end up with isn't "family product" at all. "Movies that ought to be R are being squeezed down into PG-13 in a cynical attempt to increase the potential audience," says film critic Roger Ebert of *Ebert and Roeper at the Movies.* "The G rating has been stigmatized as not being hip enough," adds Tom Ortenberg, president of Lionsgate Films.

Consider:

- *The Hulk*, the classic Marvel comic-book series, always displayed the stamp of approval from the rigid Comics Code Authority [a system of rating comic books for violence and sexual content]. Yet Universal's movie version is rated PG-13 "for sci-fi action violence, some disturbing images and brief partial nudity."
- *Sinbad: Legend of the Seven Seas*, the animated film from the makers of *Prince of Egypt*, might seem like a surefire G-rated escapade. Guess again: It is "rated PG for adventure action, some mild sensuality and brief language." Even Paramount's *Rugrats Go Wild*, based on Nickelodeon TV series *Rugrats* and *The Wild Thornberrys*, went wild enough to rate a PG for "mild crude humor."

- *Pirates of the Caribbean: Curse of the Black Pearl*, will be the first PG-13 under the Walt Disney Pictures family banner. The "action/adventure violence" (as the ratings board describes it) includes the sight of pirates slitting throats and melting down to skeletons.

While a PG-13 is much easier to market than an R, many observers say that what's getting into the category is just as strong as the R-rated films of the past. "The amount of violence and language you can get away with in a PG-13 film is amazing," says Ortenberg, one of the few studio executives who openly state their frustration with the board that others will only express privately. "A passionate scene of true lovemaking will earn an NC-17 in a heartbeat, but the brutal obliteration of a large percentage of the world's population can earn a PG."

The MPAA [Motion Picture Association of America] sponsors a yearly poll on the ratings system. In the latest edition, 76% of parents with children under 13 found the ratings to be "fairly useful" or "very useful." But a differently worded poll by the independent organization CommonSenseMedia.org found that only 21% of parents "completely trust" the ratings.

And while the big studios have become increasingly clever at shoehorning [forcing] major movies into PG and PG-13, independent companies are still getting stuck with the dreaded R, Ebert says. "Serious and thoughtful movies about teenagers are rated R, cutting them off from those they could actually serve," Ebert says. "The MPAA essentially feels violence and vulgarity are fine for PG-13, but serious consideration of sexuality is not."

A panel of Los Angeles parents administers the ratings, but Fithian says their opinions reflect different parts of the country, "and there are differences from community to community. That's why there aren't a lot of hard-and-fast rules." But there are hard-and-fast rules, argues [independent filmmaker] Samuel Goldwyn Jr. And "meanwhile, there's a picture that makes a point of telling teenagers to drive irresponsibly that got rated PG-13. More teenagers have been killed with automobiles than with sex."

Indeed, Universal's *2 Fast 2 Furious* and its predecessor, *The Fast and the Furious*, are the films most often cited by critics of ratings systems. The films glamorize illegal street racing and other criminal activity and include sex, violence and drunkenness, but they escape the R by avoiding nudity and blood. They have been blamed for the deaths of street-racing teenagers.

Tomorrow director Justin Lin [says]: "Anytime a filmmaker tries to stay true to the sensibility of today's youth, he's going to get hit with an R. Adults will say, 'Kids can't see that; that's too graphic for them.'"

—Andy Seiler

Casting the Characters

One of the problems that Lionsgate experienced with casting actors in *The Hunger Games* was the reaction of fans to the choices. As actors were announced for the major roles in the movie, there was often a huge uproar from fans. They most often complained that a particular actor wasn't physically similar enough to the way they imagined the book's characters: too short, too tall, wrong color hair, or wrong color eyes. As Collins says, "Any time you read a book and

IN FOCUS

Draft to Draft

Suzanne Collins was asked about the differences between one draft of the *Hunger Games* script and the next. She replied:

When I look at the development of the script, there was the draft I did condensing down the book—what could be cut out of it, and then filling out the backstage stories. Because in the film, we have the ability to cut away from Katniss's [perspective]. The one thing I had never been able clearly to see was not "What's the dramatic question?" Because the dramatic question is fairly forthright: Is she going to live? But it's the emotional arc that exists between Katniss and Peeta. I saw in [director Gary Ross's] draft that it was the first time it had been successfully done as an overall arc. Without it you have a film, you have a story, but you risk losing the kind of emotional impact that the film might have. And I thought, "Well, if they want me in, I have to come. I see it working now! Now they've got me and they'll be no getting out. Because I want to be in now."

get attached to the characters, to me it's always a shock when it goes from page to screen and it's not exactly what was in my head or what I was imagining it should be. So there's always that period of adjustment." Ross adds, "I really agree with Suzanne that it's wonderful that people have such a vivid image of Katniss and Peeta and Gale and they hold it so dearly. But Suzanne and I have the advantage of having seen these guys audition for these roles, and I would never judge any role or any actor until I've seen them perform it."

The first role to be cast was Katniss. The part went to actress Jennifer Lawrence. She had previously been nominated for an Oscar for her role as a tough teenager in backwoods Missouri helping to keep her family together in the 2010 movie *Winter's Bone*. Some fans felt the casting was wrong because Lawrence is not a teen and she is naturally blonde. But Collins was excited by the casting choice and even called Lawrence to congratulate her for getting the role.

Acting the part: Jennifer Lawrence was chosen as the actress to play the part of Katniss Everdeen. She was photographed here on the red carpet at the 83rd Academy Awards ceremony in 2011.

USA TODAY Life SECTION D

LIFE.USATODAY.COM

March 23, 2012

All hype breaks loose as 'Hunger Games' opens; For Jennifer Lawrence, the publicity is so much 'hecticity'

From the Pages of
USA TODAY

Jennifer Lawrence says she has invented a word to describe the electric frenzy she is experiencing as leading lady of *The Hunger Games*. "I made the word up—*hecticity*," Lawrence says. "It's all around this movie."

Devotees of Suzanne Collins's best-selling young-adult sci-fi/adventure trilogy have waited with giddy anticipation since *Hunger Games*' 2008 publication for it to be adapted for the screen. Fan websites hosted 100-days countdowns to the release of the film, distributor Lionsgate conducted fever-stoking publicity tours at malls across America, and fans camped out overnight at the March 12, 2012, Los Angeles premiere for the opportunity to scream at the film's stars as they walked the red carpet.

"Everybody has really bought into *The Hunger Games* buzz," says Jeff Bock, senior box-office analyst for Exhibitor Relations. Bock notes that *Games* "is reaching Harry Potter and Twilight proportions right now, which is amazing since it's the first movie right out of the gate. You don't often see this in the first of a series. But this is not just teenage girls pushing it. It's teenage boys as well."

The signs are everywhere. Movie ticket website Fandango.com already has crowned *The Hunger Games* as the top-selling franchise of all time based on the 2,500 showtimes that were sold out in advance. Wall Street stock in Lionsgate has soared to all-time highs.

The *Hollywood Reporter* went beyond the industry's conservative $82 million opening weekend tracking estimate and predicted in a box-office "shocker" that the movie could break the $140 million mark over the weekend. By comparison, the first installment of *The Twilight Saga* in 2008 made $70 million in its first weekend and led to the franchise's first four films earning $1 billion. (The final installment is due in November.)

Winter's Bone: Jennifer Lawrence played Ree Dolly in *Winter's Bone* (2010), a movie about family life and society in the rural Ozark Mountains of southern Missouri. The movie won Best Picture at the Sundance Film Festival, and Lawrence received an Academy Award nomination for Best Actress for her performance in the film.

"Even the expectations putting *Hunger Games* near $100 million are a huge deal," Bock says. "When you talk about that, you are talking about 'cine-magic.' People are aware this could be the next Twilight. But that might be jumping ahead of ourselves."

Director Gary Ross avoided excessive violence in the film to ensure a PG-13 rating—key to bringing in the maximum number of young fans. While the book deals with gruesome deaths, the handheld movie cameras pull away from excessive gore. "The movie is told from Katniss's point of view, she doesn't have time to gawk at the violence," Ross says. "We don't back off the violence in the book, but there's no need to indulge in it. We strike the right balance."

Ross points out that the movie was relatively inexpensive to make, with a budget estimated at $75 million to $90 million. "We know it's going to be financially successful," he says. Nonetheless, even Lawrence will be following the numbers. "I've never looked before, but I'll be watching this one," she says.

–Bryan Alexander

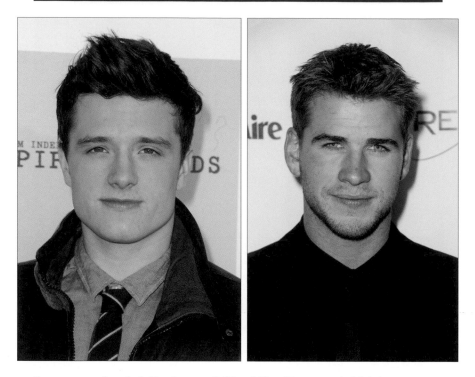

Two more roles: Josh Hutcherson *(left)* and Liam Hemsworth *(right)* were cast as Peeta and Gale, respectively. Collins was thrilled about the actors chosen to bring to life the characters in her books.

The roles of Peeta and Gale were cast next. Kentucky-born actor Josh Hutcherson was chosen to play Peeta. He has a background in television and film and got a lot of positive attention for his role as Laser, the teenage son of lesbian moms in the Oscar-nominated film *The Kids Are All Right* (2010). Australian actor Liam Hemsworth was cast to play Gale. Liam's career includes several television series as well as the movies *Triangle* (2009) and *The Last Song* (2010). He was already a good friend of Josh Hutcherson before they began filming *The Hunger Games* together. Fans debated on various Internet sites whether these actors were best for the roles. Collins firmly said that she had seen the two actors audition for the roles and that she knew they were excellent choices. About Josh, she said:

People may get thrown, say, by the color of an actor's hair or maybe something physical, but I tell you: If Josh had been bright purple and had had six foot [1.8-meter] wings and gave that audition, I'd have been like "Cast him! We can work around the wings." He was that good. That role is so key to have a boy that can use language. That's how Peeta navigates the world, that's his gift, and Josh was the one who could bring that to life in such a real and natural way.

Other cast members included well-known actors Woody Harrelson as Haymitch, Stanley Tucci as Caesar Flickerman, Donald Sutherland as President Snow, and Lenny Kravitz as Cinna. Young actress Willow Shields got the role of Katniss's sister, Prim.

More casting: Woody Harrelson *(left)* plays Haymitch Abernathy, Katniss and Peeta's mentor during the Hunger Games. Haymitch is almost always under the influence of alcohol. Katniss and Peeta's stylist, Cinna, is played by actor and singer-songwriter Lenny Kravitz *(right)*.

Panem: Abandoned houses line the streets of Henry River Mill Village in North Carolina. The setting was perfect to depict the dreary village of District 12.

Creating Panem

With the roles cast, it was also time to find a setting that could be transformed into Panem for the movie. The small town of Hildebran, North Carolina, an hour outside of the city of Charlotte, was chosen. Scouts for the movie were also interested in a small North Carolina ghost town called Henry River Mill Village, an abandoned area that still has historic buildings such as a general store. It was a perfect site to transform into District 12, Katniss's hometown.

Locals in the area were recruited as extras in the film. Some residents were worried that filming a movie in their small town would be inconvenient—with road closures and the addition of movie personnel and equipment. But others hoped that the movie would bring more money to area stores and businesses.

And . . . action!: The film crew for *The Hunger Games* shoots a scene with Jennifer Lawrence in her role as Katniss. Nearly all the film was shot in North Carolina.

Filming of *The Hunger Games* began in the spring of 2011 and continued throughout the summer. In August 2011, viewers could watch the first trailer for the movie on the MTV Music Video awards show. While fans waited for the release of the movie itself, Lionsgate bought the rights to film the second book in the series, *Catching Fire*. The film of this book is slated to hit theaters in November 2013.

Big changes: Collins made the big time after her hugely popular book series attracted fans around the world.

Looking Forward

■■■■

For years, Suzanne Collins had been immersed in writing the Hunger Games trilogy and then working on the movie. With the announcement that there would be a second movie, she knew she would be involved in creating the screenplay for that one as well.

Collins has found that her life has changed as a result of the popularity of the Hunger Games trilogy and all the attention surrounding the forthcoming movie. She recalls that she noticed this change as she was writing the final book:

I started to get calls from people I didn't know, at my home number, which at the time was listed and we had never thought anything about it. Suddenly, there was this shift. Nothing threatening happened or anything, but it is your home and you want it to be private. So I think that was the point where I felt, "Oh, something different is happening now."

Collins would have to adjust to her name being known to readers all over the world. She might not be a movie-star celebrity with a face recognizable on the street, but she was a literary celebrity. Websites cropped up about her and her books and about the Hunger Games movies. Many of the sites were created by her fans. Other fans wrote fan fiction based on the characters and themes in her books.

Collins said in a 2009 interview that her family's financial fortunes had not yet changed very much, due to the way that payments are made in publishing (slowly, over time, depending on sales). As a best-selling series, of which two books have already been purchased for movies and with one of the films coming out in 2012, chances are that the Hunger Games has been very good to Collins. Estimates suggest that she has made as much as $6 million from her books. But wealth doesn't seem to be a driving force in Collins's life.

Fame and fortune: Suzanne Collins and Cap arrive at *The Hunger Games* premiere in March 2012. Collins's books had become a smashing success. She had to learn quickly how to deal with her newfound success.

Starstruck websites just won't leave celebs alone; Anything goes except privacy

From the Pages of USA TODAY

With the popularity of gossipy websites, the schism [divide] between famous people and regular people is shrinking, yielding results that are dangerous, democratic or amusing, depending on whom you ask. Before the Internet, if average Janes or Joes spotted a celebrity engaging in something truly scandalous—say, kissing someone who wasn't his or her spouse—they'd send their scoop to a gossip columnist. But today's snarky celeb blogs have turned fans into [columnists] who might follow a star home, then post the address. Or where a star's child goes to preschool. And, per the rules of the Web, fact-checking isn't required.

What has especially aroused the ire [anger] of celebrity publicists is the newest feature on Gawker, home of 2-year-old Stalker, the user-submitted celeb-sighting column. Two weeks ago, the site began using maps to pinpoint the location of a luminary

Suzanne Collins

[famous person]. No wonder some experts believe celebrity privacy is increasingly an oxymoron [contradiction].

"A hallmark of the 21st century is going to be a complete breakdown of privacy, absolutely," says Maureen Orth, author of *The Importance of Being Famous: Behind the Scenes of the Celebrity-Industrial Complex.* "Technology guarantees it."

If a star is out in public, he or she is fair game. "The law deems you have no expectation of privacy," says Daniel Solove, law professor at George Washington University [in Washington, D.C.,] and author of *The Digital Person: Technology and Privacy in the Information Age.*

On the go: Movie star George Clooney waves off photographers in New York City in October 2011. With journalists and fans carrying cell phones that photograph and film, celebrities have little privacy.

But, industry watchers wonder, has it gone too far? Most say yes. A reporter approaching an actor is one thing, but what about a fan at Nobu eavesdropping on your sushi dinner and posting the overheard scuttlebutt, real or enhanced?

Often innocent encounters are blown out of proportion online, says Michael Joseph Gross, author of *Starstruck: When a Fan Gets Close to Fame.* Who, after all, hasn't been rude to a parking attendant or waitress once in a while? "We all have spectacularly bad days sometimes—and when we're in our 20s!" Gross says. To him, the exhaustive detailing of what a star eats or buys in public is invasive. "If you see George Clooney, you'll stare. But more than looking feels like taking. More than looking can feel like assault."

—Donna Freydkin and Olivia Barker

In a video interview, she has said that if she were to be given $1 million, she would most likely use part of it for charity and put the rest in the bank so she could always have enough money to write.

New Projects

When asked about new book projects, Collins has said that she has some ideas for a new young-adult series. And in April 2011, she told a reporter for the *New York Times* that she is writing a new picture book. She said that it would be her most autobiographical book so far and that it would use her family members' names and family photographs and illustrations. The book will most likely have something to do with the experience of a child whose parent is serving in the military, based on Collins's experience when her father was sent to Vietnam. "I specifically want to do this book, one as a sort of a memory piece kind of honoring that year for my family, and two, because I know so many children are experiencing it right now—having deployed parents. And it's a way I would like to try and communicate my own experience to them."

Vietnam War: U.S. Marines wait for enemy soldiers near the North Vietnamese border in 1966. Collins's father fought in the Vietnam War. Her next children's book will draw on her family's experience of her father's tour of duty in Vietnam.

July 19, 2011

Lu's dystopian novel is a movie in the making

From the Pages of
USA TODAY

Her mom gives her grief for loving cartoons and video games at the age of 27. But having a teenage-friendly mind is doing wonders for debut novelist Marie Lu. Though her novel *Legend* won't be released by Putnam until Nov. 29, the young-adult book is already taking a page out of *Twilight* and *The Hunger Games* with a film adaptation in the works. Lu pits teenage [characters] against each other in a near future dystopian America divided into the Republic and the Colonies. There are also trials that weed out the smartest teenagers and send those who don't make the grade off to an awful fate. Day is the male protagonist who steals to keep his family alive and revolts against the police state. June is the female military leader-in-training who blames him for a family member's death. *Legend* brings them together in conflict and for romance.

Jen Besser, Lu's editor and Putnam's publisher, says there has been a glut of similar dystopian fiction in the past year, but *Legend* stood out. She signed Lu for a three-book Legend series within weeks of her initial submission. "It's rare to find a book that is this perfect combination of action and substance," Besser says. "There's enough suspense that you're reading it and your palms get sweaty but enough depth to it that your heart breaks a little, too."

The movie deal came together mere weeks after the book was signed. *Twilight* producer Wyck Godfrey will produce *Legend,* and Jonathan Levine (*50/50*) will direct. "I felt like I was reading a Charles Dickens novel, but it happened to be set in the future," Godfrey says. "Day and June are supposed to hate each [other] and yet they fall in love. Having been blessed to experience how a strong love story can help you on the Twilight series, it's always in the back of my mind when I'm reading something."

Lu, who moved to the USA from Beijing [China] when she was 5 and now lives in Pasadena, Calif., enjoys hearing from teenagers. "I always get a kick out of hearing if they have a crush on Day or not," Lu says. "And I've heard from a couple of boys who have crushes on June. I'm always excited when the boys like it, too."

—Brian Truitt

A Day in the Life

What is a typical work-day like for Suzanne Collins? She says that she just grabs some cereal for breakfast and then sits down to work as soon as she can. Like many writers, she feels that if she has to deal with too many distractions before sitting down to write, she has a harder time focusing on the story she's working on. She tends to work for three to five hours, usually until early afternoon, before she is out of ideas. But also like many other writers, even

Mozart: Collins enjoys listening to classical music by composers such as Mozart *(above)* as she works.

when she is not actually writing, the story is moving in and out of her thoughts all day long, no matter what she is doing.

Collins listens mostly to classical music as she writes. She says that music with lyrics tends to interfere with her own thought processes and that's why instrumental classical music from composers such as Mozart works the best for her. Her two cats, Zorro and Zabel, keep her company. She and her family found the two cats as feral (wild) cats living in their backyard and rescued—or, as she says, "abducted"—them.

When asked what advice she would give to young people who want to be writers, she responds:

A lot of people tell writers to write about what they know. And that's good advice, because it gives you a lot of things to draw on. But I always like to add that they should write about things that they love. And by that I mean things that fascinate or excite them personally. *The Hunger Games* is full of things that intrigue me; you know, it's dystopia, it's got kids in it, it's gladiators, it's war, there are genetic mutations. *The Underland Chronicles* has fantasy, animals, sword fighting. And if you write about things that you feel passionately about, it is so much easier to write.

Suzanne Collins knows that her books are getting a lot of attention at the moment but that eventually her celebrity will diminish. "I'm not a very fancy person," she said. "I've been a writer a long time, and right now *The Hunger Games* is getting a lot of focus. It'll pass. The focus will be on something else. It'll shift. It always does. And that seems just fine." Until then, she is grateful that the message in her books has spoken to so many readers, both young and old. Perhaps the lessons about war and celebrity and media will reach young people and change a little about how they view their world and themselves.

Meeting the fans: During the kickoff tour for *The Hunger Games* in March 2012, actors Jennifer Lawrence *(left)*, Josh Hutcherson *(center)*, and Liam Hemsworth *(right)* visit with fans and sign autographs at a mall in Los Angeles.

As Katniss says at the end of *Mockingjay*:

Something is significantly wrong with a creature that sacrifices its children's lives to settle its differences. It benefits no one to live in a world where this happens.

Suzanne Collins's Hunger Games books show a world where brutality is the norm. But the story also shows how humans can overcome their worst tendencies. More than anything else, this hopeful message may be the most important thing of the world Collins has created.

Exceeding Expectations

The Hunger Games movie received a lot of Hollywood hype. From the moment the book was optioned as a movie, the studio built excitement about the movie. The studio wanted to keep interest in the movie high, so it gave out little bits of information. For example, fans waited eagerly for news about casting the roles. As they learned who would play which character, they shared reactions online. By the

Movie day: Excited fans line up early to see the first midnight showing of *The Hunger Games* in New York City.

last few weeks before the movie's premiere in Los Angeles, personal appearances by the movie's stars were attracting huge crowds. Many fans stayed up all night in line to get the first tickets to these events.

When *The Hunger Games* movie debuted on March 20, 2012, its popularity went beyond everyone's expectations. It had the third-highest-earning movie opening of all time, making an estimated $155 million in ticket sales. And the movie wasn't just appealing to teens. Half of the audience was over the age of twenty-five. Movie reviewers also noted that many people went to see it again to better understand the story.

Suzanne Collins liked the movie version of her book too. On her Facebook page, she wrote:

> Dear Readers,
>
> I've just had the opportunity to see the finished film of *The Hunger Games*. I'm really happy with how it turned out. I feel like the book and the film are individual yet complementary pieces that enhance one another. The film opens up the world beyond Katniss's point of view, allowing the audience access to the happenings of places . . . like *The Hunger Games* control room and President Snow's rose garden, thereby adding a new dimension to the story. The cast, led by the extraordinary Jennifer Lawrence, is absolutely wonderful across the board. It's such a pleasure to see how they've embodied the characters and brought them to life. I hope you enjoy the film!

Overall, critics liked *The Hunger Games* and felt it stayed fairly true to the book. Some critics and parents felt that the movie was still too violent for many kids to see. They said that its PG-13 rating should have been an R. Other critics feel that limiting the violence lessened the realism of the Hunger Games competition. No matter what, the hype had already begun for the second movie, *Catching Fire*!

A READER'S OVERVIEW

The Hunger Games

The first book in the Hunger Games trilogy introduces Katniss Everdeen, who lives in District 12 of the country of Panem, ruled by the Capitol district. Every year, two tributes, a boy and a girl, are chosen from each district and must fight to the death in the Hunger Games. Katniss is chosen, along with a boy named Peeta, and they fight in the Games and eventually team up. The book ends with the two refusing to kill each other to leave one clear winner.

Catching Fire

Katniss and Peeta must tour all of Panem's districts as the winners of the Games. They are also acting as a love-struck couple to explain why they refused to kill each other in the Games. Katniss finds that she is becoming a symbol of rebellion for the people of the districts. Then a special version of the Hunger

Games, called the Quarter Quell, is announced and all former winners have to fight again. Both Katniss and Peeta make it out of the arena, but Peeta is taken by the Capitol. Katniss also learns that her home district has been destroyed.

Mockingjay

Katniss is part of the rebellion, centered in District 13. Peeta gets away from the Capitol but has been brainwashed and wants to kill Katniss. Katniss sets out to kill President Snow of the Capitol. When the rebels win the war, Katniss finds out that the new president is considering reinstating the Hunger Games to punish the Capitol district. Katniss kills this new president. She is acquitted at her trial and is sent back to her ruined home district.

Peeta eventually recovers from his brainwashing. The trilogy ends with Katniss married to Peeta, and the two have children. Katniss is forever scarred by her experiences.

Gregor the Overlander (The Underland Chronicles)

The five books in this series tell the story of Gregor and his adventures in a place called the Underland, which lies beneath New York City. People called the Underlanders live in a stone city called Regalia. The area is also populated by giant versions of creatures such as rats and cockroaches. Gregor and his sister, Boots, go to Underland in search of their lost father and help the Underlanders in their war against the rats. The Underlanders believe that Gregor and Boots are the warrior and the

princess of their prophecies, who will change life in the Underland and help defeat various enemies.

TIMELINE

1962: Suzanne Collins is born in Hartford, Connecticut.

1968: Her father is deployed to the war in Vietnam. Later, the family lives in Belgium while he is stationed there.

1980s: Collins attends college at Alabama School of Fine Arts, followed by graduate school at New York University. She marries Cap Pryor, and eventually they have two children, Charlie and Isabel.

1991: Collins begins writing children's television shows.

2001: She receives a Writers Guild of America award for writing the children's television special *Santa, Baby!*

2003: Author James Proimos urges her to write a children's book.

  Collins's first book, *Gregor the Overlander*, is published.

2004: *Gregor and the Prophecy of Bane* is published.

2005: *Gregor and the Curse of the Warmbloods* is published.

2006: *Gregor and the Marks of Secret* is published.

2007: *Gregor and the Code of Claw* is published.

2008: *The Hunger Games*—the first in a trilogy of novels for young adults—is published.

2009: *Catching Fire*—the second book of the Hunger Games trilogy—is published.

  Lionsgate purchases rights to make a movie of *The Hunger Games*.

2010: *Mockingjay*—the third book of the Hunger Games trilogy—is published.

  Suzanne Collins is named to *Entertainment Tonight*'s Entertainers of the Year list.

2011:   Lionsgate purchases the rights to make a movie of *Catching Fire*.
        The Hunger Games movie begins filming.

2012:   *The Hunger Games* movie is released.

2013:   *Catching Fire*, the movie, is scheduled to be released.

GLOSSARY

dystopia: an imagined place or state of things where people live in a state of repression and control. The leaders of this type of society work to give the impression that the control and repression are for the good of society.

gladiator: ancient Romans trained to fight against other men or wild animals in an arena, usually for public entertainment

labyrinth: a maze made from complicated or irregular pathways and passages that make it difficult to find the way out

lottery: a process of choosing or deciding an outcome through random selection

tactics: actions that are carefully planned to achieve a specific goal

utopia: an imagined place or state of things in which everything is perfect. For example, in a utopian society, all laws, government, and social conditions are perfect.

SOURCE NOTES

5 Scholastic, "Lionsgate Feasts on the Hunger Games," *Scholastic Media Room*, March 17, 2009, http://mediaroom.scholastic.com /themes/bare_bones/opk/lionsgate_hungergames.pdf (July 4, 2011).

5 Lisa Hirsch, "Jennifer Lawrence Cast as Katniss in 'Hunger Games,'" *ET Online*, March 17, 2011, http://www.etonline.com /movies/108871_Jennifer_Lawrence_Cast_as_Katniss_in_Hunger _Games/index.html (July 4, 2011).

9 Scholastic, "The Hunger Games," *Scholastic Media Room*, n.d., http:// mediaroom.scholastic.com/hungergames (July 4, 2011).

10 *School Library Journal,* "Suzanne Collins: The Hunger Games," Starred Review, Suzannecollinsbooks.com, n.d., http://www .suzannecollinsbooks.com/the_hunger_games_69765.htm (July 6, 2011).

13 Susan Dominus, "Suzanne Collins's War Stories for Kids," *New York Times*, April 8, 2011, http://www.nytimes.com/2011/04/10 /magazine/mag-10collins-t.html?pagewanted=all (July 4, 2011).

16 Hannah Trierweiler Hudson, "Q&A with Hunger Games Author Suzanne Collins," *Scholastic.com*, 2011, http://www2.scholastic .com/browse/article.jsp?id=3754859 (July 4, 2011).

16 Book Report, "Author Profile: Suzanne Collins," *Teenreads*, August 2010, http://www.teenreads.com/authors/au-collins-suzanne.asp (July 4, 2011).

26 Ibid.

29 Hillel Italie, "How Has Hunger Games Author Suzanne Collins Life Changed?" *Huffington Post*, September 23, 2010, http://www .huffingtonpost.com/2010/09/23/hunger-games-suzanne -collins_n_736441.html (August 28, 2011).

30 Jen Rees, "Suzanne Collins Interview," suzannecollinsbooks.com, n.d., http://www.suzannecollinsbooks.com/events.htm (July 4, 2011).

31–32 Ibid.

32 Ibid.

32–34 "Suzanne Collins Works," *suzannecollinsbooks.com*, n.d., http:// www.suzannecollinsbooks.com/gregor_the_overlander__book _one_in_the_underland_chronicles_48384.htm (July 4, 2011).

34 Book Report, "Author Profile."

37 Ibid.

38 Scholastic Canada, "Suzanne Collins' Classical Inspiration," *Scholastic Canada*, n.d., http://www.scholastic.ca/thehungergames/videos/ classical-inspiration.htm (July 10, 2011).

39 Ibid.

44 Book Report, "Author Profile."

44–45 Ibid.

46 Suzanne Collins, *The Hunger Games* (New York: Scholastic Books, 2008), 371.

48–49 Scholastic, "Praise for The Hunger Games," *Scholastic Media*, n.d., http://mediaroom.scholastic.com/themes/bare_bones/opk/ hungergames_reviews.pdf (July 11, 2011).

49 Ibid.

50 Dominus, "Suzanne Collins's War Stories."

50 Elissa Petruzzi, "To the Death: Suzanne Collins Kills," *RT Book Reviews*, September 2009, http://www.rtbookreviews.com/ magazine-article/death-suzanne-collins-kills?page=1 (August 27, 2011).

52 Dominus, "Suzanne Collins's War Stories."

52 Rebecca Reid, "The Hunger Games by Suzanne Collins," *Rebecca Reads*, June 21, 2010, http://reviews.rebeccareid.com/the-hunger -games-by-suzanne-collins/ (August 27, 2011).

58 Hudson, "Q&A."

61 Scholastic, "Hunger Games Contest," *Scholastic.com*, n.d., http:// scholastic.com/thehungergames/contest/ (June 8, 2012).

63 Petruzzi, "To the Death."

63 Ibid.

63–64 Book Report, "Author Profile."

66 Dominus, "Suzanne Collins's War Stories."

67 Suzanne Collins, *Mockingjay* (New York: Scholastic, 2010), 390.

70 Petruzzi, "To the Death."

73 Karen Valby, "Team Hunger Games Talks," *Entertainment Weekly*, April 7, 2011, http://insidemovies.ew.com/2011/04/07/hunger -games-suzanne-collins-gary-ross-exclusive/ (July 10, 2011).

73   "A Message from Suzanne Collins about the Hunger Games Script," *The Hunger Games Trilogy Fansite*, June 4, 2011, http://www.hungergamestrilogy.net/2011/06/a-message-from-suzanne-collins-about-the-hunger-games-script/ (July 23, 2011).

74   Valby, "Team Hunger Games Talks."

78   Ibid.

78–79   Ibid.

83   Ibid.

87   Italie, "How Has Hunger Games Changed?"

90   Maryann Yin, "Suzanne Collins Writing 'Most Autobiographical Work to Date,'" *Galleycat*, April 11, 2011, http://www.mediabistro.com/galleycat/suzanne-collins-writing-most-autobiographical-work-to-date_b27510 (August 28, 2011).

93   Hudson, "Q&A."

93   Book Report, "Author Profile."

94   Collins, *Mockingjay*, 77.

SELECTED BIBLIOGRAPHY

Baines, Emily Ansara. *The Unofficial Hunger Games Cookbook: From Lamb Stew to "Groosling"—More Than 150 Recipes Inspired by The Hunger Games Trilogy.* New York: Adams Media, 2011.

Book Report. "Author Profile: Suzanne Collins." *Teenreads*, August 2010. http://www.teenreads.com/authors/au-collins-suzanne.asp (July 4, 2011).

Dominus, Susan. "Suzanne Collins's War Stories for Kids." *New York Times*, April 8, 2011. http://www.nytimes.com/2011/04/10/magazine /mag-10collins-t.html?pagewanted=all (July 4, 2011).

Dunn, George A., Nicolas Michaud, and William Irwin. *The Hunger Games and Philosophy: A Critique of Pure Treason:* The Blackwell Philosophy and Pop Culture series. New York: John Wiley, 2012.

Egan, Kate. *The Hunger Games: Official Illustrated Movie Companion.* New York: Scholastic, 2012.

———. *The World of the Hunger Games.* New York: Scholastic, 2012.

Gresh, Lois H. *The Hunger Games Companion: The Unauthorized Guide to the Series.* New York: St Martin's Press, 2011.

Hirsch, Lisa. "Jennifer Lawrence Cast as Katniss in 'Hunger Games.'" *ET Online*, March 17, 2011. http://www.etonline.com/movies/108871_ Jennifer_Lawrence_Cast_as_Katniss_in_Hunger_Games/index.html (July 4, 2011).

Hudson, Hannah Trierweiler. "Q&A with Hunger Games Author Suzanne Collins." *Scholastic.com*. 2011. http://www2.scholastic.com/browse /article.jsp?id=3754859 (August 28, 2011).

Petruzzi, Elissa. "To the Death: Suzanne Collins Kills." *RT Book Reviews*, September 2009. http://www.rtbookreviews.com/magazine-article /death-suzanne-collins-kills?page=1 (August 27, 2011).

Roback, Diane. "'Mockingjay' to Conclude the Hunger Games Trilogy." *Publishers Weekly*, February 11, 2010. http://www.publishersweekly .com/pw/by-topic/childrens/childrens-book-news/article/42030 -mockingjay-to-conclude-the-hunger-games-trilogy-.html (July 22, 2011).

Scholastic. "The Hunger Games." *Scholastic Media Room*. N.d. http://
mediaroom.scholastic.com/hungergames (July 4, 2011).

Scholastic Canada. "Suzanne Collins' Classical Inspiration." *Scholastic Canada*.
N.d. http://www.scholastic.ca/thehungergames/videos/classical-
inspiration.htm (July 10, 2011).

Seife, Emily. *The Hunger Games Tribute Guide*. New York: Scholastic, 2012.

Springen, Karen. "'Catching Fire' Catches Fire," *Publishers Weekly*, May 28,
2009, http://www.publishersweekly.com/pw/by-topic/childrens
/childrens-book-news/article/17137--catching-fire--catches-fire.html
(March 8, 2012).

FURTHER READING AND WEBSITES

Books

Bailey, Diane. *Suzanne Collins*. New York: Rosen, 2012.

Grundell, Sara, and Nia O. Cajayon. *Fame: Suzanne Collins*. New York: Bluewater Productions, 2012.

Hoover, Elizabeth. *Suzanne Collins*. Farmington Hills, MI: Lucent, 2012.

Krohn, Katherine. *Stephenie Meyer: Dreaming of Twilight*. Minneapolis: Twenty-First Century Books, 2011.

Lankford, Ronnie D. *At Issue: Reality TV*. Farmington Hills, MI: Greenhaven Press, 2008.

Llana, Sheila. *How to Analyze the Works of Suzanne Collins*. San Francisco: Essential Library, 2012.

Orwell, George. *1984*. 1949. Reprint, New York: Plume Books, 2003.

Sexton, Colleen. *J. K. Rowling*. Minneapolis: Twenty-First Century Books, 2008.

Wilson, Leah. *The Girl Who Was on Fire: Your Favorite Authors on Suzanne Collins' Hunger Games Trilogy*. Dallas: Benbella Books, 2010.

Websites

Hunger Games Movie
> http://hungergamesmovie.org/
> The official website for the *Hunger Games* movie has information about the movie's filming, trailers, podcasts, and the releases of the *Hunger Games* and *Catching Fire* movies.

Hunger Games Trilogy: Unofficial Fansite
> http://www.hungergamestrilogy.com/fansite/official.php
> This fan-created site offers information about the *Hunger Games* books and movies, and links to other sites, activities, and quizzes.

Liam Hemsworth
> http://liamhemsworth.com/
> On this blog-style site, fans can learn more about Liam Hemsworth, the Australian actor who plays Katniss's love interest Gale in *The Hunger Games*.

The Official Jennifer Lawrence Website
http://jenniferslawrence.com/
Visit the website of Jennifer Lawrence, who portrays Katniss in *The Hunger Games* film. On the website, fans can learn more about her background, send and follow fan mail, view photos, and enjoy trailers.

The Official Website of J. K. Rowling
http://www.jkrowling.com
J. K. Rowling, the author of the phenomenally successful Harry Potter series, has a great website for learning about her books for young readers, her current projects, and her new novel for adults.

The Official Website of Josh Hutcherson
http://joshhutcherson.com/
Watch trailers, enjoy photos, and learn more about Josh Hutcherson's life and work. Hutcherson plays Peeta, the male tribute from Katniss's district, in *The Hunger Games.*

The Official Website of Stephenie Meyer
http://www.stepheniemeyer.com
Stephenie Meyer's official website contains information about her past and present projects as well as biographical information about this author of the popular Twilight saga.

Suzanne Collins Author Website
http://www.suzannecollinsbooks.com/index.htm
Collins's official author website includes a biography, list of books, reviews, and an author interview.

The Twilight Saga
http://www.thetwilightsaga.com/
This is the official online destination for fans of the Twilight series. On the site, Twilight fans can get information and video clips related to the books and the films and much more.

INDEX

PHOTO ACKNOWLEDGMENTS

The images in this book are used with the permission of: AP Photo/Victoria Will, pp.1, 86, 88 (bottom); © Michael Hurcomb/CORBIS, pp. 3, 6 (bottom); © Todd Strand/ Independent Picture Service, pp. 4, 6 (top), 14, 18, 24, 32, 33, 35, 43, 48 (background), 51, 53, 59, 62 (top), 64, 65, 68, 76, 80, 88 (top), 91, 96 (both), 97 (both); © Ray Tamarra/FilmMagic/Getty Images, p. 5; © Eric Charbonneau/WireImage/Getty Images, pp. 7, 74; Murray Close/© Lionsgate/Courtesy Everett Collection, pp. 8, 72; © Rob Schumacher/USA TODAY, pp. 9, 49 (right); © Todd Plitt/USA TODAY, pp. 10, 60, 62 (bottom); © Margaret Bourke-White/Time & Life Pictures/Getty Images, p. 12; U.S. Air Force Photo, p.15; Library of Congress, pp. 16 (LC-USZ62-10610), 47 (LC-USZ62-69671); © Nancy Kennedy/Dreamstime.com, p. 17; © Sara D. Davis/USA TODAY, p. 19; © ruimleal/Flickr/Getty Images, p. 20; © Anthony Shaw/Dreamstime. com, p. 21; Franklin D. Roosevelt Presidential Library, p. 22; Maggie Wilson-PHOTOlink.net/Newscom, p.23; Courtesy Everett Collection, pp. 25, 27; TM and Copyright © 20th Century Fox Film Corp. All rights reserved/Courtesy Everett Collection, p. 26; © Splash News/CORBIS, p. 28; © Universal Images Group/Getty Images, p. 29; © Martin Molcan/Dreamstime.com, p. 31; MCT/Newscom, p. 34; U.S. Army/Air Force Staff Sgt. Samuel Bendet, p.36; © NHPA/SuperStock, p. 37; © DEA/G. Dagli Orti/De Agostini/Getty Images, p. 39; Lionsgate/Newscom, pp. 40 (all), 41 (both); © DEA/A. De Gregorio/De Agostini/Getty Images, p. 42; AP Photo, p. 45; © Monty Brinton/CBS Photo Archive/Getty Images, p. 46; AP Photo/Matt Peyton, p. 48; © Allison V. Smith/USA TODAY, p. 49 (left); ©iStockphoto.com/Juanmonino, p. 56; © Toei Co. Ltd./Courtesy Everett Collection, p. 57; Jaap Buitendijk/© 2011 Warner Bros. Ent. Harry Potter publishing rights © J.K.R. Harry Potter characters, names and related indicia are trademarks of and © Warner Bros. Ent. All rights reserved/Courtesy Everett Collection, p. 67; Jeff Malet Photography/Newscom, p. 70; © Frederick M. Brown/ Getty Images, p.73; © Jeff Vespa/WireImage/Getty Images, p. 79; Sebastian Mlynarski/© Roadside Attractions/Courtesy Everett Collection, p. 81; © Frazer Harrison/Getty Images, p. 82 (left); © Jordan Strauss/WireImage/Getty Images, p. 82 (right); © Dan MacMedan/USA TODAY, p. 83 (left); © Kevin Kane/WireImage/Getty Images, p. 83 (right); © Justin R. Anderson, p. 84; © Murray Close/Lionsgate/Photofest, p. 85; © Gregg DeGuire/FilmMagic/Getty Images, p. 87; © Alo Ceballos/FilmMagic/ Getty Images, p. 89; AP Photo/Horst Faas, p. 90; © DEA/A. Dagli Orti/De Agostini/Getty Images, p. 92; © Jesse Grant/Getty Images, p. 93; AP Photo/John Minchillo, p. 94.

Front cover: Maggie Wilson-PHOTOlink.net/Newscom.

Back cover: © Todd Plitt/USA TODAY.

Main body text set in USA TODAY Roman Regular 10.5/15.

ABOUT THE AUTHOR

Marcia Amidon Lusted is the author of more than sixty nonfiction books for young readers, as well as hundreds of magazine articles. She is an assistant editor for Cobblestone Publishing and a writing instructor. She is also a pianist and accompanies several school choral groups. She lives in New Hampshire with her family.